GETTING READY FOR A GREAT RETIREMENT

A PLANNING GUIDE

Barbara Deane

A MINISTRY OF THE NAVIGATORS
P.O.BOX 35001, COLORADO SPRINGS, COLORADO 80935

The Navigators is an international Christian organization. Jesus Christ gave His followers the Great Commission to go and make disciples (Matthew 28:19). The aim of The Navigators is to help fulfill that commission by multiplying laborers for Christ in every nation.

NavPress is the publishing ministry of The Navigators. NavPress publications are tools to help Christians grow. Although publications alone cannot make disciples or change lives, they can help believers learn biblical discipleship, and apply what they learn to their lives and ministries.

Library of Congress Catalog Card Number: 91-67286
ISBN 08910-96620

Some of the anecdotal illustrations in this book are true to life and are included with the permission of the persons involved. All other illustrations are composites of real situations, and any resemblance to people living or dead is coincidental.

Printed in the United States of America

To Douglas, my husband,
whose retirement made this book
not only possible, but necessary.

CONTENTS

INTRODUCTION

About a year ago, my husband made a troubling announcement. He had just discovered that, after the following year, his company would no longer pay the entire cost of medical insurance for retirees. Such an expense could reach staggering proportions.

And so, with this unknown future expense looming before us, we decided we might be better off financially if he retired at age sixty-two rather than at age sixty-five. Suddenly retirement, instead of being a distant four years down the road, was now only one year away.

So I did the only normal thing: I panicked.

From the time you begin working in America, money is deducted from your paycheck for Social Security. You know you'll be retiring one day—but nobody ever tells you that it could arrive so unexpectedly.

There's so much to think about. Will there be enough money, now and in the future? How will our health be affected by advancing age? Should we move? How will retirement affect our marriage?

Frankly, I was worried. Retirement was clearly going to change my life. Our income, for example, would be cut drastically. And retirement even had the potential to change our marriage in ways I couldn't imagine. I didn't really think Doug was likely to become one of those retired husbands who tries to take over management of the household, spending his days inventorying the canned goods . . . but *I didn't know this for sure.* I envisioned myself trying to write while a bored and restless husband rattled around the house.

I was concerned for my husband—perbaps more than he was for himself. Like most men of his generation, Doug has always led a compartmentalized life. His home and family have been his retreat from problems at work. And when family problems seemed overwhelming, he could always lose himself in his work. At retirement, his almost-lifelong means of coping was going to disappear. Instead of home and work, there would now be only home. This was going to be an enormous adjustment for him.

But whatever the problems, we were not going to be the only ones facing them. Retirees now number close to 10 percent of the population. By 2025, this figure may be closer to 25 percent. If present trends (longer life expectancy and a lower birthrate) continue, in the year 2025 Americans over sixty-five will outnumber teenagers by more than two to one.

Two-thirds of all the people in the entire history of the world who have lived beyond the age of sixty-five are alive today. Children born in the closing years of this century can expect to spend up to one-third of their lives in retirement![1]

If there are going to be this many retirees, I reasoned, there must be information out there that I could discover and share. And so I began researching various dimensions of retirement. I found plenty of books covering *some* of the areas of retirement, but none that adequately looked at the full spectrum.

And so the idea for this book was born.

HOW TO USE THIS BOOK

From time to time, we all need to step back and look at our values, priorities, and goals in life. Is what we're doing meeting our needs and carrying us toward our goals? If not, we may need to make some changes. What better opportunity than during the retirement years—or, just as timely and beneficial, *before* the retirement years—to do this kind of in-depth searching?

While individuals can certainly benefit from reading this book, I hope you will go a step further with it. If you are married, you and your spouse could do as Doug and I did:

Read each chapter together and discuss the questions at the end. Single persons could do the same thing with a friend. Or the questions could be used as discussion starters for small group meetings of retirees and pre-retirees. If there are no small groups like this where you live, why not start one?

I've tried to make this a different kind of retirement book. I realized early in my research that many people make decisions about retirement based on financial pressure, peer pressure, or even media (advertising) pressure, and then find out that they are locked into situations that do not meet their deepest physical, psychological, and spiritual needs. I had hoped that Doug and I could avoid making that mistake in our own lives by looking *first* at our needs, *then* trying to build a lifestyle that supports them—rather than vice versa. For that reason, you'll find all sorts of concerns—about yourself, your use of time, your family, your relationships—before the chapters about the financial dimension.

My philosophy is that you can always find a way to finance your true needs, if only you know what they are. (Maybe not all your *wants*, but hopefully your needs. There is a difference.)

Retirement planning can become a true voyage of discovery. There are many aspects that need to be considered. Let's begin.

PART ONE

RETIREMENT: THE FIRST DAY OF THE REST OF YOUR LIFE

CHAPTER ONE

GETTING TO KNOW ME

I'm not sure that people really know who they are.
Ken Fors, Retirement Counselor

What makes one retired person contented and another one miserable?

"I've wondered about this a lot," said Dave, a happy retiree for over five years. "I see some guys who are having a ball. But then there are the others who are going downhill. You don't see them on the golf course anymore. Then they stop coming to the monthly club dinner meetings. Pretty soon, you can't get them out of the house."

Many of these men were quite happy in their younger days. On top of the world. So what happened? You have to wonder if there is perhaps some difference in the qualities that are needed to be a successful older person compared to being a successful younger person.

MOST OLDER PEOPLE ARE HAPPY
A survey commissioned by the Marriott Corporation of 1,000 senior Americans from all walks of life is reassuring to those who may be fearful about what lies ahead in their retirement years:

- 96 percent of those surveyed said they were happy.
- 82.8 percent said they were useful members of society.
- 79.2 percent said they were *not* bored with life.
- 75.3 percent said they felt financially secure.

The Vaillant study of Harvard graduates indicates that there *is* a significant difference (see page 29). Qualities such as sociability that led to happiness in youth no longer seem to lead to happiness as these men age.

RETIREMENT: A NEW IDENTITY CRISIS?

All our adult lives, we've derived most of our self-worth from the roles we play. A woman looks in the mirror and says, "I'm a wife, a mother, a teacher. Yes, but *who am I* when these roles in life are over?" This is the question that everyone has to face sooner or later.

Challenges to our identity can come at any time. I was talking to a young woman in her thirties who had injured her knee in a skiing accident. "Suppose my knee doesn't heal and I have to give up skiing?" she wondered out loud. "How would that make me feel about myself?" Her identity as a strong, self-reliant, athletic person was at risk. She was forced to ask herself, *Can I give up skiing and still be me?*

This is the kind of question that faces all of us at retirement age: Could I give up ______________ and still be me? (Fill in the blank with anything you value—your work, some favorite possession, your home, your prowess as a tennis player, your good looks, your position as a church leader or community volunteer—anything that is of great importance to you.)

Obviously, this will not be the same for everyone. If you've never been much of an athlete, the loss of agility and strength in your body may not be a very great loss. If you were never a raving beauty, the loss of your youthful good looks may not be that much of a threat. If your job was just a means of earning a living to you, then being forced to give it up on retirement could come as a relief.

But for many people, their work *is* their total identity. A few years ago, my husband attended the funeral of a coworker his own age (mid-fifties). Most of the people there were company people.

"Thank you for coming," the man's adult son said with tears in his eyes. "He lived for this company. It was his whole life!"

My husband came home from the funeral saddened and quite shaken. He realized clearly that this was not something he'd care to have said at his own funeral: "He gave his whole life for his job." Wasn't this man also a husband, a father, a neighbor, a friend, a citizen? Evidently not. He lived only for his work. Imagine how difficult he would have found retirement to be. Work was his only means of identity.

Retiring from a job in a culture that defines everybody by what they do for a living has to be an identity crisis. Yesterday you were a judge or a bond salesperson or a social worker or a policeman or a teacher or an electrician, and today you're . . . nobody. Or are you?

REDISCOVERING YOURSELF

When your work life ends, you may have to rediscover yourself. After all, how can you plan your life after retirement if you don't really know this person you're planning for?

The mature adult needs to disengage from his old roles in order to rediscover who he was meant to be. As Eugene Bianchi said, "One must first get in touch with one's true inner voices, which may have been stifled or ignored in the busy years of youth and midlife."[1]

These voices might be very deeply buried. Psychologist Eda LeShan declares that "most of us grew up believing that it was more important to be good than to be ourselves." Why did we reach that conclusion? Because when we were children, "being good" meant pleasing our parents. To displease them was to risk losing their love. "To a certain extent every child 'sells out' for love."[2]

"ACTIVITY" IS NOT THE ANSWER

Many of us may believe that our only value is in what we do. We may feel we have to keep earning love by *doing*, not by *being*. Such a singular focus leads to a life of constant activity.

Many guidebooks to retirement, and many retirees themselves, emphasize "keeping busy" as the key to successful retirement. But mere "busyness" can become a distraction that prevents us from discovering who we really are. Instead of plunging into activities, it might be more helpful during pre-retirement or the early retirement years to undertake retreats, peer discussion groups, self-exploration via the arts, or other creative paths to help us get in touch with our being—who we are when we're not doing something to meet other people's expectations. Then we might discover activities that express our true selves and bring us joy.

In addition to allowing ourselves to plan in a practical way for the future, we need to allow ourselves to dream. Many of us may have forgotten the importance of dreaming, imagination, creativity, playfulness.

WHY PLAY IS SO MEANINGFUL

By "play," I don't mean frivolity or childishness. I mean any activity undertaken for its own sake, without thought of reward.

For some people, this can happen only after retirement when, as a retired business executive put it, "I realized I couldn't fail anymore." It took him a couple of years to adjust to the idea that a person could actually enjoy activities in which there is no winning or losing. When you no longer have to prove anything, when you no longer have to compete for status, prestige, or promotions, then even work can become play.

Without using the word *play*, Dave, the contented retiree I mentioned at the beginning of the chapter, was referring to this element of playfulness when he called his retirement activities "passions." ("Hobby isn't a strong enough word," he said.) A passionate interest in Chinese porcelains sent him to auction houses and antique shops, libraries and art museums, talking to collectors and art historians, utterly fascinated by a subject that, only a few years before, he had never known existed.

His knowledge will not make him one whit richer, younger, or more lovable. He has this passionate love for collecting Chinese porcelain for its own sake—a luxury that few people can afford when they're busy earning a living.

"USEFULNESS" DOES NOT DEFINE OUR WORTH

This spirit of playfulness reminds us of the dignity and worth of human life itself. This dignity is "unconditional," says Viktor Frankl, an Austrian psychiatrist who survived the Auschwitz death camps. "It must not be confounded with mere usefulness in terms of functioning for the benefit of today's society—a society that is characterized by achievement orientation and consequently adores people who are successful and happy."[3]

Unless we learn to redefine "success," unless we learn to value being and not just doing, unless we truly believe that people are valuable even when they are not useful, we will be tempted after retirement to become depressed by our own "uselessness," or allow society to make us feel diminished because we're no longer "productive."

TWO STAGES OF RETIREMENT AGE

"Retirement" is usually not one stage of life, but two. The first is what gerontologists call a "young old" stage of active, independent living that can vary greatly in length. The second is an "old old" stage of declining health and growing dependence. A realistic retirement plan cannot assume that the "young old" stage will last indefinitely. Yet, say the experts, most people spend more time planning for a two-week vacation than they do for retirement.

Some of the other challenges of retirement in the nineties that nobody tells you about are:

- Aging parents who need care
- Adult children who need help
- Coping with children's divorce and remarriage
- Having to raise your grandchildren
- Widowhood and remarriage

Retirement as an endless vacation is a myth that the marketplace tries to sell us. This is no vacation! In reality, it could be the most stressful period of our lives. How in the world will we meet all these challenges? The only answer that makes any sense to me is to build up our inner resources and not be lulled into thinking that there are no storms ahead. But what is it that we need to learn?

WINNING RETIREMENT ATTITUDES

"I used to think money was the most important thing to plan for when you retire. Now I know it's not so. Some of these guys who are falling apart have a lot more going for them financially than I ever will," Dave said.

If money is not the answer, then what is? Dave thinks it has something to do with attitude.

What kind of "attitude," for example, makes for successful retirement and aging? Something else that Dave said gives us an important clue: "When I retired, I made up my mind never to go back and visit my old office. I saw what happened when people tried it. Nobody had time to talk to them—they were too busy working—and you don't fit in anymore. You become a fifth wheel."

Dave didn't say this with either bitterness or regret in his voice. As a realist, he'd accepted it as a fact of life. He met old friends from work and other retirees from his company socially, but he knew better than to try to hang on to his former role and the relationships that went with it.

One key to a successful old age as well as a successful retirement is this ability to *let go* of whatever roles you can no longer keep. People who are able to do this draw on the inner strength that comes from the knowledge that there is much more to the human personality than the roles we play.

QUESTIONS FOR DISCUSSION

1. What do you look forward to most about retirement?
2. What do you fear most about retirement?
3. Name one talent or interest that you had to give up or set aside in order to earn a living. Can you go back to it? Do you want to?
4. Name at least one activity that you do for pure enjoyment.

CHAPTER TWO

LETTING GO

"Whoever wants to save his life will lose it."
Jesus Christ, Matthew 16:25

A good friend of mine named Bonnie lives alone in a small apartment. By just about anyone's standard, she is poor. Her present circumstances are in sharp contrast with her past life as the wife of a successful mining engineer. She was once a world traveler, amateur anthropologist and archaeologist, radio personality, and author.

A series of difficult events changed the entire course of Bonnie's life. A disastrous fire suddenly took her beautiful house in Hawaii with its lifetime of treasures, many of them from her travels with her husband. Then, after she nursed her husband through a long, difficult illness that used up all their savings, she herself was worn down. Now, at the age of eighty, her health is quite precarious. She has survived several operations.

When I visited her just before Christmas, it was obvious that she had not been sitting around feeling sorry for herself. Her little apartment was piled high with homemade Christmas gifts and letters. She was waiting for her next Social Security check to arrive so that she would have the money to mail them.

Bonnie has tried to get people at the senior center where she's a volunteer to take an interest in writing to people in the military service. "Some of them say that they can't afford the postage," Bonnie told me with exasperation in her voice. "But they spend more money on cigarettes every month than I do on postage. It's not lack of money; it's what you choose to do with what you have."

TRYING TO HANG ON

Contrast Bonnie with another retiree we'll call Howard who is fast turning into a bitter old man. Howard was the Sunday school superintendent of his church for over twenty years. Everybody depended upon him and he began to think of himself as irreplaceable.

But health problems made it impossible for Howard to continue running the Sunday school as he used to. There was no backup because he'd always done everything himself. The church board asked him to help them find and train a successor, but he found one excuse after another not to do so.

Finally, because the program was not being handled effectively any longer, the board had to ask Howard to step down. This upset him unbearably. He has had a lot to say about the church's "ingratitude" for all he's done over the years. Howard has nothing but criticism to offer his successors, and he's even thinking of leaving the church.

Bonnie was forced to let go of her husband, her affluent lifestyle, her home, and her health. Yet her life still had purpose and value because her primary focus was on what she could contribute now, not on what she had lost. The people who hang on to what is gone forever just can't seem to trust God to give them something new. They have to defend this thing that they've always had, that they've always done. They cling tenaciously to it, because they see this as their only security.

"HANGING ON" CAUSED BY FEAR

People who hang on too long frequently destroy churches, because while they can no longer physically do the necessary work, they still want to call the shots. These people also destroy family businesses because when they "retire," they still interfere and want to make decisions. They wreck family relationships because they want to run their adult children's lives as if they were still responsible for them.

Hangers-on live in fear of losing whatever gives their lives meaning. But by clinging to the old and familiar out of fear, they miss whatever new blessings and meaning God may have for them.

But fear is a choice. We can choose love instead. We can choose service. We can choose hope. We can choose to let go of old tasks and old roles. Usually, the best way to let go of old roles is to step into new ones. Retirement is an ideal time to think about the vast possibilities.

An important question a retiring person must ask is this: *What new roles can I take on that will be even more exciting than the ones I'm giving up?*

These choices are not made once and for all on the day we retire. Letting go is a lifelong task, one we've had plenty of practice in. By the second year of life, almost all of us had to let go of the security of crawling in order to stand up and walk. At age six, we had to let go of the security of home as we went off to school. In adolescence, we let go of the security of being our parents' little children in order to become adults and take on adult responsibilities.

Sometimes it's a gradual process. Letting go of our children, for example, begins when they're quite young and may not be completed until they've been adults for some time.

WE GAIN ONLY BY LOSING

Letting go never ends. In middle age, for example, each of us needs to let go of our former competitiveness in order to relate to younger people as their mentors and guides. If we continue to treat young people as rivals, we opt for stagnation and frustration. (Eventually, some young rival is bound to get us, anyway!)

Howard could have trained his successor and gracefully turned over the reins of his church program to someone else. But he didn't. He made a choice, and that choice made him miserable—although he blamed someone else for what happened to him, which is typical of hangers-on.

So it goes throughout life. Each new stage requires us to decide to give up some present security from an earlier stage. It's never easy and it's never over. Letting go of our work when we retire is just the first of many late-life relinquishments. Yet letting go is a necessary first step before we can gain *the blessing we are meant to have in the next stage of life.*

"AGEISM" RUNS RAMPANT

■ "Ageism" is prejudice—unthinking negative opinions about people based solely on their age. A Harris poll taken in 1981 revealed that older people have just as many false, negative stereotyped beliefs about the aged as the rest of the U.S. population. Older people seem to think that *they're* the ones who are the exceptions to their peer group.

■ Eighty percent of the people over sixty-five surveyed said that they had enough money to live comfortably through their retirement years. But the same group guessed that 50 percent of the people over sixty-five were living in poverty. This is not true.

■ Twenty percent of the people over sixty-five said they had a chronic illness. But they guessed that 50 percent of the people over sixty-five had debilitating health problems. This is also not true.

■ Only 5 percent of people over sixty-five are in some kind of institution, such as a nursing home. But the people over sixty-five who were polled thought that 20 to 25 percent of the over-sixty-five population was institutionalized.[1]

Most of us get so many negative attitudes about aging from our society that we have trouble imagining there is anything to be gained in old age. To believe that really takes faith!

When *we* were the younger people, faith in ourselves often carried us through. We thought, *Because we met the previous challenge successfully, we can do this, too!* But in our later years, the challenges become greater just as our powers are lessening. It's then, when we are inadequate, that we need to trust the Power greater than ourselves, a benevolent and loving God who will not fail us. How can we walk away from a job when we retire without looking back, unless we can believe that God has something better for us than what we're giving up?

CONNECTING WITH THE ETERNAL

Those who take the time to research older adults tell us that the happiest ones are those who have found some life purpose in something or someone outside of themselves. Not all of these people are conventionally religious by any means. Some have devoted their lives to a cause that we would not necessarily agree with. But they have solved the problem of getting beyond selfishness.

Or to put it another way: *One's selfish little ego is not a sufficient basis on which to sustain a meaningful life in old age.* You can get away with a self-centered perspective more easily when you're younger. But the loss of status and income that usually accompanies retirement tends to bring all of us face to face with our own spiritual poverty. There is a great need to connect, even if we have never done so before — with Something or Someone who is not, as we are, about to die and pass away.

The temporary nature of human life is wonderfully expressed in the first chapter of Ecclesiastes:

> "Meaningless! Meaningless!"
> says the Teacher.
> "Utterly meaningless!
> Everything is meaningless!"
> What does a man gain from all his labor
> at which he toils under the sun?
> Generations come and generations go,
> but the earth remains forever.
> (Ecclesiastes 1:2-4)

At first glance, these words may seem like the disillusionment of a cynical old man. But it's something more than that. It's a detachment from a purely human view of life and an identification with human life from God's point of view. From the vastness of time and space, anything that man accomplishes in a short lifetime is going to seem puny indeed. This can easily lead to despair. But we move beyond despair when we are able to see our lives as a significant part, however small, of some larger plan. When this happens, we find it a little easier to let go of our self-centeredness.

GETTING AND SHARING WISDOM

The freedom of the retirement adventure gives us an opportunity for one of the greatest tasks of advancing years: getting and sharing wisdom. Wisdom is not something that comes automatically with age. (We all know people who are old but *not* wise.) According to the book of Proverbs, it's a gift from God. It's not based on intellectual ability; even simple people can be wise. It's more of an ability to see the big picture. A sense of proportion. Knowing your own limitations. Knowing what's important in life, and what's trivial.

Many older people confuse wisdom with knowledge and experience. Because they've been around longer and have encountered the same problems in the past, they think younger people should take their advice and avoid making the same mistakes they did. But giving unasked-for advice is the very opposite of wisdom! The wise thing is knowing when to speak and when to keep silent.

As difficult as it is to define, we all know wisdom when we see it. Older people who have it don't have to *do* anything. You just want to "hang out" with them, be near them, bask in their glow. Becoming that kind of attractive old person is well worth giving up some of the things we valued in our youth.

THE GAINS THAT COME WITH AGE

Some things in life are a joy to get rid of. I've already mentioned one: competitiveness. If you can give that up, you gain a richer, more rewarding relationship with others based on sharing.

What else would we be better off without? What would happen if, while we were still middle-aged, we began to work at letting go of some of the following things we tend to hang on to?

The need to always be right. Then we would find it easier to forgive and be forgiven.

The need to be needed (if this is the means by which we try to control and manipulate people). Then we would find it easier to respond to other people's *real* needs freely and joyfully.

The need to believe that we know everything. Then we could become eager learners all our lives.

The need to defend our illusions. (We all have lies we tell ourselves—for example: my parents were perfect, my marriage is idyllic, I was an ideal parent to my children.) Then we would not waste precious energy defending ourselves from the truth, and God would find it easier to get through to us.

The belief that we own anything, either property or people. It never was ours anyway—it was only on loan for a little while. Then we could give it back to God, its rightful owner, with a grateful heart.

The need to keep up with the latest fashions—whether it's a fad in clothing, hairstyles, or the latest trendy idea. Then we could sort out what's eternal from what's only temporary.

Old resentments and hurts. Then we could be healed.

Being perfect. Then we could be human. As a friend of mine observed, "I used to be perfect, but it was a drag!"

Rigid sex roles and stereotypes. Then we could develop important but neglected parts of our personalities, instead of trying to live up to society's expectations of what the ideal man or a woman "should" be.

The need to be independent at all costs. Then we would be stronger—it takes a strong person to admit he or she is weak enough to need help. And as a result we could also discover the joy of community.

The need to please other people. Then we might learn to please God, who wants us to serve Him by being ourselves.

QUESTIONS FOR DISCUSSION

1. What would be the most difficult thing in your life to give up?
2. What would you most like to gain as you grow older?
3. Have you ever encountered prejudice because of your age? Do you have any of these "ageist" stereotypes yourself? If so, how can you overcome them?
4. Do you feel like part of something larger than yourself? What would increase that feeling?

CHAPTER THREE

PLANNING TO GROW

Change is inevitable, but growth is optional.
Anonymous

In older, traditional societies, before there were written records, the wisdom of the tribe resided in its elders. *They* were its books. Their memories, reaching back into the past, were the tribe's only means of continuing into the future. The tribal culture was passed down from generation to generation. Even today, certain older people in Japan who have mastered unique ancient skills are designated "national treasures," and are subsidized by the government.

ELDERS OF THE TRIBE

In our modern world there are still "elders of the tribe,"[1] but they may go unrecognized. On the island of Maui in Hawaii, my husband and I hiked in Io State Park up to Tablelands. Suddenly, as we came out from a thicket of small guava trees into an open space, there was a tall older man whose kindly brown face was set off by a shock of snow-white hair. He was removing the invasive, non-native guava trees and replanting endangered native trees.

Nobody was paying him. He was doing this in his spare time and at his own expense. As he put it, "I'm doing what I believe in."

A native of Maui, he was on intimate terms with the natural environment, collecting seeds in the wild and growing the plants at his home until they were large enough to be set out where they can survive. Occasionally someone helps him, but for the most part he works alone. At age sixty-five, he may not live to see the trees he is planting reach maturity, but he acts on the unselfish belief that future generations will benefit from what he is preserving, even if he can't.

Is it possible for *you* to be an "elder of the tribe"? I think so. Anytime we act unselfishly, working for a future we will never see, we play this very necessary but very underrated role.

In our society, so dominated by technology, where new things are valued and old things are considered obsolete, retirees are tempted to withdraw in order to avoid rejection for being "outdated." But we need to learn to value what we have to share with younger generations. Never apologize for being old. Start by banishing the phrase "over the hill" from your vocabulary.

LEARN TO VALUE YOURSELF

I have a recurring fantasy. Sometime in the twenty-first century, an electromagnetic catastrophe knocks out all the microwave ovens on the globe. Panic sets in. People are starving because nobody knows how to cook real food. At that point I am found, and I'm led out, doddering but still mentally alert, into a makeshift kitchen. Aha! I remember how to cook with an "old-fashioned" oven. I demonstrate a few simple techniques and prepare some outstanding dishes. The world is saved! I am a heroine! Now I can die.

This is farfetched, I know. But you don't have to wait for a catastrophe to occur to become an elder of the tribe. The world is already a catastrophe. If you have found the secrets to having love, joy, and peace in your heart, if you know how to make a marriage work or how to get along with people who are different from you, then realize that the world desperately needs that kind of wisdom. It's selfish for us to shut ourselves off from younger people and refuse to give them the benefit of our years.

LOVE IS THE WISEST THING OF ALL

If the world needs more love, retired people who have more time would seem to be the logical ones to provide it. But will we?

The key issue of retirement is not finances, not living arrangements, not filling our time constructively. The key issue is finding an answer to the question that haunts our hearts: "Will anybody love me when I get old?"

It's sometimes hard to believe that anybody could. You may remember an old song called "There'll Be Some Changes Made." One of the lines says, "Nobody loves you when you're old and gray" and most of us have bought into that philosophy.

Older people are just as prejudiced about aging as anybody else. Just ask yourself, "Do I believe that older people are unlovely, ugly, stupid, slow, unproductive, and worthless? Do I believe that I'm like that, or will be some day?" If you actually think that nobody can love you, you'll find it much more difficult to show love. And it will be much safer to continue to relate to people in the only way you know how: by controlling them through the use of power and manipulation.

Do you recall the story of Shakespeare's *King Lear*? When he was king, everybody pretended to love him because they feared his power. When he gave away his kingdom to his daughters and became powerless, he was treated with contempt. Aren't we all afraid of becoming like King Lear if we give up our power?

WHAT PREDICTS HAPPINESS AT RETIREMENT?
George Vaillant, M.D., of Dartmouth Medical School and his wife, Carolyn O. Vaillant, MSSW, have studied a group of Harvard graduates since they were college sophomores in 1940. These men have now reached sixty-five. The Vaillants were interested in what factors predicted "life satisfaction" (that is, happiness) at age sixty-five. Their findings, not too surprisingly, were that the most reliable predictors were (1) absence of alcohol abuse, (2) absence of mood-altering drug use, and (3) maturity of ego defenses.

"Ego defenses" are the coping mechanisms we all use when we're threatened by life's problems. Some examples of mature ego defenses are sublimation (improving by finding substitutes), suppression (postponing gratification), altruism, and humor. Examples of immature ways of coping include projection (blaming others), passive-aggressive behavior (procrastination, avoidance), and acting out.

It's interesting that all of these predictors were in place by the time these men were fifty.[2]

Yet we need to give love as much as the world needs to receive it. In doing so we do *not* give up any "power." If anything, we gain in the only *real* power in life, which is a *humble* kind of power. These will be the last years we will have to heal old hurts—both those we've received and those we've inflicted—to forgive and be forgiven, to love and be loved, before it's too late. The greatest wisdom of all is to seize this opportunity.

CAN PEOPLE CHANGE?

Yes, but perhaps your response is, "I'm too old to change." Or you may believe, "That's just the way I am. People don't change their whole personality." Yes, they do. Researchers have found that the people who age successfully have radically changed their outlook on life and their value systems from what they were when they were younger.

We do know that people age at different rates and that much of how well we age physically is determined by genetics. Drs. Gerald McClearn and Robert Plomin, behavioral geneticists at Pennsylvania State University, have been studying 350 sets of Swedish twins over sixty who were raised in separate homes. They've found substantial genetic influence later in life—in personality, mental health, biomedical function. But what really surprised them were the two things *not* influenced by heredity.

Those two factors are a person's *attitude* toward what happens to him or her in life and *agreeableness*—the ability to get along with people. Almost every other personality trait they tested (emotionality, impulsiveness, shyness, etc.) is influenced to some extent by heredity.

What this means is that the two key elements in how well we age are the easiest to change because they're in no way predetermined by our genes. If we change out attitude toward what happened to us earlier in life, we can significantly alter our outlook on life for the better. This is very good news.

A FRUITFUL OLD AGE

In the Bible, a long life is considered to be a gift from God, and *personal growth throughout one's life span is to be expected.*

> The righteous will flourish like a palm tree,
> they will grow like a cedar of Lebanon;
> planted in the house of the LORD,
> they will flourish in the courts of our God.
> They will still bear fruit in old age,
> they will stay fresh and green. (Psalm 92:12-14)

I take this to mean that the old are still growing in character, growing spiritually. The fruit that they bear is the fruit of the spirit: love, joy, peace, patience, kindness, goodness, faithfulness, gentleness, self-control (Galatians 5:22). These have nothing to do with biological age.

The older we get, gerontologists say, the more diverse and individual we become. Whatever you were when you were young, you will tend to become "more so" as you age. If we're negative and bitter now, we're going to get worse, not better. If, on the other hand, we seek spiritual growth, we can expect to have it. We are pilgrims and discoverers all our lives.

Retirement is the ideal time to begin working on our attitudes. Now that we're not working, we have more time. Yet we also realize that our remaining time on earth is limited.

SPIRITUAL TASKS OF LATER LIFE

Some spiritual tasks carry on throughout life—for example, the need to love and be loved, to forgive and to be forgiven. But some are unique to the later years:

- Letting go of old roles.
- Adjusting to the losses that come with age.
- Valuing being over doing.
- Valuing wisdom over physical prowess or beauty.
- Coming to terms with one's own life story.
- Preparing for death.

THE GIFT OF MORTALITY

Some scientists talk about extending life as if living forever was something to be greatly desired. But think about it. If you knew your present life was going to go on indefinitely, could you endure it? Wouldn't it be unbearably tedious, boring, and painful? Imagine two hundred years of television reruns! Ten thousand more meals to prepare. Descendants in the hundreds whose birthdays you'd have to remember. Everlasting arthritis in your joints.

Viktor Frankl reminds us, in the following passage, how death gives meaning to life:

> Imagine what would happen if our lives were not finite. . . . Wouldn't we be justified in postponing everything—nothing would have to be done today, for we could do it as well

> tomorrow, next week, next month or next year, postponing it *ad infinitum*. Only under the threat and pressure of death does it make sense to do what we can and should, right now. That is, to make proper use of the moment's offering of a meaning to fulfill—be it a deed to do, or work to create, anything to enjoy or a period of inescapable suffering to go through with courage and dignity.[3]

By retirement age, we should no longer be trying to pretend that our lives will go on forever. If we need to become wiser, to do more forgiving, to show more love, or to fulfill some heart's desire, we can no longer postpone these tasks, for we no longer have endless years to fritter away.

Yet if we talk about tasks to be done, we also need to talk about the grace we can receive to do them. These years are not a sentence, filled with grim duties to be performed, but a pure gift. We are the first generation in history to know that we will probably be given many years beyond what was normally considered "old" in the past.

Our generation of retirees is better educated, more affluent, and in better health than any previous generation. What we do could very well be significant. We could be the pioneers who redefine retirement and aging for many generations to come.

QUESTIONS FOR DISCUSSION

1. What new role or roles do you envision for yourself after retirement?
2. Think of some person older than yourself that you admire. What is his or her secret?
3. Think of another older person that you wouldn't want to be like. What can you do to avoid becoming like this person? (Or did he or she really have a choice?)
4. Which of the positive methods of coping are you strongest in (see box on page 29)? In which do you need more work?
5. What are some other coping methods that are not listed?
6. What spiritual tasks of old age do you expect to find most difficult? Why?

PART TWO

SPENDING THE GIFT OF TIME

CHAPTER FOUR

TIME FOR EXPLORATION AND DISCOVERY

"What'll we do with ourselves this afternoon?" cried Daisy. "And the day after that, and the next thirty years?"
F. Scott Fitzgerald, *The Great Gatsby*

This morning, I passed a camper parked in our neighborhood with a licence plate that said "RETIRED" in large letters. Surrounding this word in smaller letters were "No mortgage, no paycheck, no worries, no responsibilities." Retirement for this person must be like the exhilarating experience of a child getting out of school for summer vacation.

FREEDOM: IT'S GREAT . . . OR IS IT?

But these feelings don't last for a schoolchild. Soon the elation of summer freedom is followed by wearying boredom. Time hangs heavy on our hands. Then it's back to school to start the cycle all over again. Except for retirees. This is *it*!

One retired man complained to me as he set off to go fishing one morning, "The only thing wrong with retirement is that I can't take a vacation from it." I sensed that he was only half-kidding.

If retirement equals freedom from all responsibilities, we're in trouble. Responsibilities anchor us to life on planet earth. If nobody needs me, I may be unnecessary.

So freedom is wonderful, but freedom should be more positive than negative—freedom to contribute something new and unique, not just freedom to get away from all my troubles in the world. We are given a marvelous gift of time in retirement. It's surely a gift of freedom. The question is, *How will we use it?*

Every retirement counselor I've interviewed has his collection of horror stories about people whose "dream retirements" turned sour. I met one of these people myself on our vacation in Glacier National Park. He'd retired to Upper Michigan for the fishing, he said. That was a few years ago. Now the fishing is terrible. Too many people moving in. Too much development. Too many *other* fishermen. Not enough *fish*! Another retirement dream bites the dust.

NO TIME TO SHIFT GEARS

"The long trip" is often first on a retiree's agenda—the reward one gives oneself for a lifetime of hard work. But at the end of this vacation, the question of "*Now* what do I do?" still remains. No transition, no planning, has taken place since leaving the world of job and "responsibilities."

At an Elderhostel in Hawaii, we met an active couple in their early sixties. This was their *nineteenth* Elderhostel trip since his retirement two years before. In between, they'd taken several cruises. Their daughter, who was expecting her first child that year, had begged them to stay home for a couple of months around her due date.

It seemed to me that unless these two were going to spend the rest of their lives as aging Flying Dutchmen, sooner or later they would have to make some decisions. But for the moment I had the distinct impression that the male half of the couple, at least, wasn't ready to face his own retirement.

Pre-retirees desperately need transition time to ease the terrible adjustment of going suddenly from overwork to none at all. Yet a surprisingly small percentage of people put forth the time and effort necessary to come up with a good plan.

In generations past, when aging farmers slowed down, they would gradually turn more of the farm responsibilities over to their sons. In the Old Testament, the Levites (the priestly tribe) at the age of fifty were supposed to "retire from their regular service and work no longer. They may assist their brothers in performing their duties at the Tent of Meeting, but they themselves must not do the work" (Numbers 8:25-26). Note that the Levites did not retire to inactivity. Apparently, they were to have "second careers" as teachers and advisors to the younger men.

Most modern employers, however, do not let workers ease out of their work responsibilities gradually. My husband, for example, is working so hard at his job that even if he delayed retirement for three more years, he'd be no better prepared for it then than he is now. He's had no chance to explore some of his retirement dreams to see if they will really work out.

A TRANSITION THAT WORKED

It's unusual to meet a couple like Don and Margaret, who found a new occupation in their late middle years and made the transition into retirement without missing a beat. Don had owned a successful auto leasing and rental business, but in his late fifties he went through a life-changing experience that made him more interested in people than in things. And so he embarked on a new course.

Don received training from his church's denomination and, with his wife and another couple, began giving weekend workshops at churches throughout the Northwest. Gradually, as this new interest in church work took hold, Don turned more of his business over to his son, and eventually sold it to him.

Another one of their sons is an ordained pastor. By the time Don and Margaret were ready for retirement in their early sixties, they were prepared in every way (including financially) to work without pay, calling on church visitors, teaching, making hospital calls, and facilitating small groups in their son's church. Eventually, they plan to train their replacements, work themselves out of a job, and move on. This phase of their lives has a purpose that evolved over a period of time. There was no sudden stopping and starting. But I'm afraid they're the exception, not the rule.

NEEDED: A NEW PURPOSE

Retirement as it is now practiced in the United States encourages people who have worked too hard without leisure for thirty or forty years to believe that they "deserve" to spend the rest of their lives doing nothing. But the words of theologian and mystic Thomas Merton give a more enterprising and realistic perspective:

> There are some men who seem to think their acts are freer in proportion as they are without purposes, as if a rational

> purpose imposed some kind of limitation upon us. That is like saying that one is richer if he throws money out the window than if he spends it. . . . . As for freedom, according to this analogy, it grows no greater by being wasted . . . but is given to us as a talent to be traded with until the coming of Christ. In this trading, we part with ours only to recover it with interest. We do not destroy it or throw it away. We dedicate it to some purpose, and this dedication makes us freer than we were before. Because we are freer, we are happier. We not only have more than we had but we become more than we were.[1]

SOME PEOPLE MAY *NEED* TO WORK

If retirement is forced on someone rather than sought out by that person, it *is* harder to face. The whole experience of retirement then takes on the character of unemployment, accompanied by all the negative feelings of worthlessness, depression, and grief that being fired or laid off typically brings.

Some people work only because they need the income. But work also fills many other needs in our lives. It keeps us out in the world and in contact with other people. It makes us feel useful, a part of some larger purpose. Contributing to society raises our self-esteem. Work keeps us mentally alert and emotionally balanced. It may even improve our physical health.

"My father feels so much better," a young friend told me. His seventy-two-year-old dad had been hired by a large department store chain to do telemarketing. He now has a reason to get up and get out of the house every day. In Atlanta, the Metropolitan Atlanta Rapid Transit Authority (MARTA) has hired retirees to work at the turnstiles during rush hours, giving directions and keeping an eye on the flow of traffic. At my favorite Jack in the Box restaurant, the lunch hour traffic is "hosted" by an elderly man who greets me at the door and bows to me both coming and going. These jobs may be far below the status level of these people's pre-retirement employment, but that dimension is offset by the psychological benefit of being out in the world and in contact with people.

ACTIVITIES THAT MEET YOUR NEEDS

An exercise that may help you raise your consciousness about the meaning of your own activities comes from a pre-retirement course given under the auspices of the National Council on Aging. It asks you to list ten activities you enjoy. It then asks you to rate these activities, on a scale of 1 to 10, according to how much they benefit you in the following areas: self-esteem, social interaction, fun, creative expression, adventure, physical fitness, emotional satisfaction, mental stimulation, and income production.

There are no right or wrong answers. What is enough social stimulation for one person may be quite inadequate for another, depending on how you define it. One "benefit" not on this list that you might want to add is "serving God."

If you are not yet retired, rate your work according to each of these categories. You may be surprised at how many benefits you receive from working. Such a major personal lift makes it difficult for many recently retired people to find an adequate substitute for their job without going through a long period of adjustment. It explains why some go back to work even if they don't need the money. Interesting volunteer work that fulfills as many needs as your former job may be very difficult to find.

Going through this exercise may also help you spot areas of your life that are out of balance. I found that my activities were light in meeting my needs for socializing and for physical fitness. So perhaps in retirement I should look for activities that would get me out meeting people or help me become more physically active.

This exercise should help you answer these questions: *What activities do I need in retirement to replace what I'm doing now? What activities would make my life richer, fuller, and in better balance?*

Most people take at least a year to adjust to the sudden changes that retirement brings. During this time:

1. *Allow yourself to dream – but test your dreams against reality.*
2. *Give yourself time to explore available options.*
3. *Allow yourself time to adjust.*
4. *Don't rush into anything you can't easily get out of.*
5. *Don't become discouraged if the first things you try don't work out. Try something else.*

Needless to say, married retirees must talk over these dreams and make their plans together. I love the story of the couple who went through pre-retirement counseling together. When asked about retirement plans, the husband announced, "I plan to travel a lot."

The wife commented, "Well, take plenty of postcards! I'd like to hear from you often."

Obviously, travel was *not* an important part of her future plans. You can't assume that your spouse has no individual, personal needs. Do not make plans *for* your spouse, but rather *with* your spouse.

A SMORGASBORD OF IDEAS

The following chapters in part 2 present a smorgasbord of ideas that today's retirees can choose from. Don't be intimidated by them: there are more here than you could try in a dozen lifetimes. The purpose is simply to give you some suggestions and idea starters. Most successful retirees put together a balanced lifestyle of volunteer work, education, and leisure (including travel). Some include paid work (usually part-time) as well. Even if you do work for pay after retirement, you don't have to continue doing what you were doing before if you don't want to. Retirement gives you much more freedom to try something new, and to fit work into *your* schedule, instead of vice versa.

After you have given some thought to what you might want to do with your retirement time, *then and only then* should you consider whether you want to move after retirement. *Where* you spend this gift of retirement time is just as crucial a decision as *how* you spend it.

QUESTIONS FOR DISCUSSION

1. Do you view retirement negatively (i.e., "Now I can stop working") or positively (i.e., "Now I can start doing _____," fill in the blank with your own plans)?
2. What are your dreams for life after retirement?
3. How will you "test" these dreams in real life?
4. Have you shared these dreams with your spouse?

CHAPTER FIVE

VOLUNTEERING: FINDING YOURSELF BY GIVING YOURSELF AWAY

Life is like a ten-speed bike.
Most of us have gears we never use.
Charles Schulz, Creator of *Peanuts*

When I think about retired people who seem not to know what to do with themselves, a scene from my childhood flashes into my mind. In my memory, I am returning home from school. I come around the corner, and my heart skips a beat when I realize that police cars and ambulances line our block.

A few doors from our house, our neighbor—a balding, middle-aged man—sits on a kitchen chair on the front lawn. He is sobbing. Every window of his house is standing wide open. It seems that the man's wife has attempted suicide by turning on the gas.

But this story has a happy ending. The woman was childless and didn't work outside the home (please remember, this was 1942). Her husband, an officer in the merchant marines, was absent for months at a time. After her unsuccessful suicide attempt, the wife received therapy. She returned to an earlier interest in art and sewing, and within a few years she was making beautiful stuffed animals and dolls that were in great demand.

"I never knew I could do it," she said.

What a near tragedy! It took a suicide attempt to lead her into developing her God-given talent.

There are many retirees in a similar situation, their unknown talents withering away from lack of recognition and use. We all have gears we never use.

TAKE THE QUEST SERIOUSLY

What a wonderful opportunity at retirement to discover and use both the talents we *know* we have and also the new abilities and interests we have not yet discovered! When you're old, you probably won't regret the things you *did* do. You'll regret the things you *didn't* do.

If you don't need to earn a living, then you are free to use volunteer work as an opportunity to expand your horizons—to grow and develop yourself, as well as serve others. In order to do this, you need to use the same type of self-assessment you would use if you were a young person just starting a career. However, unlike a young person, you have a lifetime of experiences to draw on, and more abilities than you would be able to use in any one volunteer position.

So, you have to make choices. Take your time to make solid decisions. You may even want to consider using a vocational counselor, or a counselor who specializes in pre-retirement planning (that is, someone who is trained in psychology or sociology, not a financial planner).

DOES IT PAY TO VOLUNTEER?

Volunteering may not pay in financial rewards, but volunteers will tell you that it surely does pay them in personal satisfaction. It puts a whole new zest into their lives. Recently, social scientists have conducted studies and report that volunteering raises people's self-esteem. Altruism is good for you. This should come as no surprise to you and me. Two thousand years ago, Jesus of Nazareth said, "It is more blessed to give than to receive" (Acts 20:35).

It's also more *fun* to give than to receive. That's an important factor. The same criteria should be used for finding a volunteer job as for finding a paid job. But it should definitely be something you enjoy. You also need to decide, "Do I want to do something that's like my old career, or do I want something that's a complete change of pace, something that meets a need in my life my former career didn't?"

Retirees can easily transfer their skills to a new setting. Clare, a former first-grade teacher, is now teaching bridge to senior citizens. Bill had been in sales. He was no longer interested in selling and he didn't need an income, so he put his "people skills" to use by volunteering to train volunteers for a community crisis hotline.

VOLUNTEERING IN RETIREMENT

Are older volunteers different from their non-volunteer peers? Yes. Volunteers tend to be more socially active, belong to a larger number of voluntary associations, have less time to spare, and more easily find ways to fill whatever free time they do have. They miss working less than non-volunteers. Those with part-time jobs are more likely to volunteer than those who are not working.

Seventy percent of volunteers attend church one or more times each week, compared to 50 percent of non-volunteers. Women tend to volunteer much sooner after retirement than men. Many men volunteer because of their wives' encouragement.

Volunteers perceive their own health as better than non-volunteers, even though by objective standards it is no better. Volunteers are more involved in caring for other family members, go to restaurants more often, spend more time in recreational activities and hobbies, read more, and socialize more with friends, neighbors, and relatives. Non-volunteers spend more time in passive and solitary pursuits—watching TV, sitting and thinking, and doing nothing.

AN EXERCISE IN LISTING AND PRIORITIZING

My husband and I went through an exercise together that helped us a great deal. You might also find it helpful. In doing this exercise, give yourself permission to dream a little. Be creative!

Make a list of all your interests, not necessarily in the order of importance. Then make a list of the skills you've built up over a lifetime. Don't ignore ordinary survival skills that you might take for granted, such as household budgeting, driving a car, telephoning, shopping, or cooking. Then look at both lists. Connect your skills list and your interests list with lines to give you some clues about areas of volunteer work that might be of interest to you.

When Doug and I got finished, our lists looked something like these:

My Lists

INTERESTS	SKILLS
Outdoors	Writing
Gardening	P.R./Marketing
Cooking	Teaching/lead workshops
Nutrition/exercise	Organizing/leading small groups
Hiking	Thinking up ideas
Reading	Communicating
Kids (especially grandkids)	Household management
Small groups	Shopping
Travel	
Writing	

Doug's Lists

INTERESTS	SKILLS
Hiking/backpacking	Teaching
Canoeing	Small group leader
Travel	Problem-solving
Teaching	Computer
Small groups	Showing love to elderly
Christian living	Making people feel wanted
Visiting sick and elderly	Leading/organizing
Reading	Insurance (work skills)
Baking bread	
Grandkids	

You may find, as we did, that some items are on both sides of our lists. Teaching, for example, may be both an interest *and* a skill. You may also find that you have listed skills you're really not that interested in using any further. So be sure to rank your interests and skills in order of importance.

For example, I listed household management as a skill, but my interest in either doing this for someone else or teaching it is close to zero. Similarly, Doug is fairly sure he doesn't want to do anything with his knowledge of insurance after he retires, even though he is interested in teaching and realizes that teaching what you know is often a natural transfer into a new retirement activity.

But he does enjoy visiting the elderly in nursing homes,

something most people find very uncomfortable. He could certainly do that in retirement. "But," I suggested, "why not use more of your skills? You could get more training and then train other volunteers in the techniques you use."

"The thing I do most at work is problem-solving," he said. "I think I'd like to do something like that."

Then he learned about ombudsmen in nursing homes. These are the people who try to work out problems that nursing home patients are having. Now all he needs to do is get the necessary training, then find someone who'd like him to volunteer to do this.

I don't think we need to worry about whether he will be welcomed as a volunteer. In the past, most volunteer work was done by married women who did not work outside the home. Today, their places have been largely taken by retirees. If it weren't for us, many of the nonprofit organizations we depend on wouldn't get their work done!

WHAT DO *YOU* WANT OUT OF IT?

There are certain questions you need to ask yourself before you embark on the path of volunteering: What do I want to get out of a retirement activity that's missing in my life now? Fun? Creativity? Being with people? Do I like working with children? If so, what age? What about young adults? Elderly people? Could available volunteer opportunities meet any of these needs?

But finding the right volunteer work is often just as difficult as finding a paid job. You don't know what's available. Organizations don't know how to reach you. Also, many organizations under-utilize volunteers. Today's retirees are more educated and skilled than retirees were a generation ago. They don't always want to sit and stuff envelopes.

Some communities may have a central clearinghouse for volunteer work. In my community, the Volunteer Bureau publishes a newsletter listing community agencies' volunteer needs. Recently, it advertised for volunteers to (1) assist with sports and activities at a local high school, (2) lead tours of a local history museum, or (3) teach arts and crafts at a local nursing home. Perfect for someone who likes sports (and teens!), history, or art.

Not all of the volunteer jobs they list call for a long-term commitment. Sometimes it's only for a few hours—to host a charity fund-raising party or hand out T-shirts at a fund-raising marathon.

How do you find out about these opportunities if your community doesn't have something like our local Volunteer Bureau? Nationally, AARP has a volunteer talent bank. You register, fill out a form, and the computer matches your skills with available volunteer positions. Intercristo has a similar program for both paid and unpaid positions in church and parachurch organizations. The AARP service is free; Intercristo charges a fee. Or you can contact any of the other organizations listed in the resource section for this chapter.

CREATE YOUR OWN SOLUTIONS

One innovative response to the problem of matching volunteers to available opportunities is The Center for Creative Retirement's Senior Leadership Seminars given at the University of North Carolina at Asheville. These are eight-day sessions in the history, culture, politics, economics, and social structure of the community, bringing together retirees and community leaders. The retirees become aware of community problems. Frequently, they do something about them. One retiree, for example, organized a Seniors in the Schools project to bring older volunteers into the classroom.

The SLS program has been so successful in Asheville that it has been expanded to eight other North Carolina localities. (A similar project, Retirees in Leadership, is sponsored by the National Retiree Volunteer Center in Minneapolis.) University of North Carolina has begun giving workshops about how to start an SLS to representatives of other colleges and universities, so perhaps we'll see this idea expand.

IDEAS TO SPARK YOUR CREATIVITY

Retirees are doing or planning so many creative activities that it's impossible to list them all. But here are some examples that might just challenge you in your areas of interest and skills.

Bob Wingfield, who loves the outdoors, became a docent at a children's natural history and science museum. (A docent is someone who leads tours and explains the exhibits.)

Mary and Bill Riley, who love to camp, are volunteer campground hosts. They host at a different national or state park every summer.

Bill Foster, a retired contractor, sets aside time every so often to help build homes for the poor through Habitat for Humanity.

Dick Sullivan, a financial industries executive, plans to set up his own volunteer financial consulting service when he retires. Through his church, he's met many young couples who are having problems with their personal finances, or who want to start businesses. He has the expertise they need.

Many retired businessmen gravitate to SCORE (Service Corps of Retired Executives). SCORE especially wants to recruit more women and minorities. In 1990, SCORE provided over 700,000 hours of free counseling to small business people in the United States. Over 86,000 people attended 2600 SCORE business development workshops during the same period.

VOLUNTEERING AND TRAVEL

Many organizations, including church and religious organizations, offer volunteers the opportunity to travel to distant and exotic places (but usually at your own expense). You no longer have to take a vow of poverty and dedicate your entire life to enter a mission field either at home or abroad. Short-term volunteer programs use any willing worker who can spare as little as a week. Seniors in good health are more than welcome.

Last year, our friends Martin and Helen Hight spent two weeks in Sweden helping to build a new building on a Bible school campus under the auspices of Greater European Missions (GEM). Costs are kept low; and travel and other out-of-pocket expenses are tax-deductible.

Most people think they're going to Third World countries to give, but find that they receive far more.

"You definitely get outside your comfort zone," says Marilyn Shaver. "You gain so much respect for these people and their culture."

Marilyn and her husband, Bill (both retirees), have made short-term mission trips to Papua, New Guinea, to Mendenhall, Mississippi, and to a small village in Guatemala. This year they will lead a team of a dozen people from their church—ranging in age from twenty-eight to seventy-two—to Guatemala City to work on building a school.

"We're housed in dormitories in bunk beds, and we do our own cooking," Marilyn said. The work is hard, Marilyn emphasized, and you will not have the comforts you're used to at home.

"But it's life changing!" Marilyn said. "Warn people that if they don't want to change, stay home."

Working eight hours every day side by side with the villagers, they built and almost completed a community center from the ground up. Every evening, they had a program, including Bible study. People came from the village to visit, and with the help of an interpreter, the two cultures were able to communicate.

Bill and Marilyn attended village church services, and visited schools and homes. No special skills are necessary in this kind of work, according to Marilyn. The sponsoring organization (which in Guatemala was World Concern) sends a representative, and a local supervisor at the work site hands out work assignments every day.

A SAMPLING OF PROGRAMS

Is there anywhere in the United States or in the rest of the world that you've always wanted to visit? Going there as a volunteer will enable you to experience the country through the eyes of the people. Have you always had a secret yen to be an archaeologist, or to go under the seas like Jacques Cousteau? Have you ever wanted to be a cowboy? Believe it or not, there's a program to match almost every interest.

Earthwatch, for example, places volunteers with research scientists in archaeology, marine biology, animal behavior, ecology, and anthropology projects around the world. The Heifer Project uses volunteers at its ranch near Little Rock, Arkansas, to help raise livestock for low-income families throughout the world.

The American Hiking Society places volunteers in national parks for the summer season in a variety of positions. The U.S. Forest Service has similar opportunities in national forests. So do some state parks. How would you like to spend a month in Alaska? With a commitment of four weeks or more, volunteers receive training, uniforms, and sometimes housing and food-expense stipends. Would you like to help lead Sunday worship services in national parks? An organization called Christian Ministry in the National Parks might have something for you.

Teachers are needed as longer-term volunteers by Los Ninos, an organization supporting orphanages in Mexican border towns.

The Sioux Indian YMCA needs experienced recreation leaders for its summer camps. If you have professional skills in medicine—doctors, nurses, optometrists, dentists, etc.—or in engineering or agriculture, many organizations would be interested in you.

One of the most popular volunteer travel opportunities for retirees inside the U.S. is MAP (Mobile Assistance Program). Retirees take their RVs to work sites to construct or renovate buildings for churches or church camps. Friends camp out together as a group, and it becomes a great social occasion as well as a service that saves churches thousands of dollars.

WHAT ABOUT THE CHURCHES?

While more people of retirement age in the U.S. belong to churches than to any other single type of organization, the churches have been slow to challenge their retired members to go beyond routine "church work." Whenever Christians have taken the lead in establishing new ministries, retirees have been an essential part of the team—whether it's by serving meals to the homeless, building houses for the poor, providing respite for caregivers, helping the frail elderly maintain their independence, tutoring children, or working with refugee families. Churches need to be more conscious of this natural, built-in people resource.

Instead of being part of the solution for an aging population, many churches and religious institutions are part of the problem. Instead of seeing the elderly as "aging prophets," the church, like the rest of society, tends to see aging as a punishment and avoids it.

Churches need to become a vigorous counterculture that will not only care for their aging members but support the changes people need to undergo as they age. We need to practice the ethic of love and caring that we preach.

Three main areas of need are (1) guidance in the ethical issues raised by aging and suffering (death and dying, intergenerational justice, etc.), (2) better programs for aging members, especially intergenerational programs, and (3) helping individuals grow spiritually as they age.

CELEBRATE AGING

One retired member of a large California congregation said to me, "This church offers something for every age group—except ours!" Look at your church budget. How much money is earmarked for ministries to older adults? I know, the older people may say, "We don't need anything. Spend the money on youth work. Young people are the future."

This perpetuates the myth that the old have no future. But it also overlooks the fact that concentrating so much attention on young people gives them nothing to look forward to. For their sake as well as ours, aging needs to be presented as something worthwhile.

Ceremonies that *celebrate* retirement and aging would be an important first step. Since the Bible speaks of the fortunate old as achieving three-score-and-ten years, age seventy might be an appropriate age for an extended celebration, says Henry C. Simmons, Director of the Center on Aging at the Presbyterian School of Christian Education. Also needed, he believes, are celebrations in honor of longtime church members, expressing thanksgiving and gratitude.

Sister Patricia Murphy, a leader in ministries to the elderly, suggests that in addition to retirement ceremonies, a church could hold a "missioning to aging" ceremony, commissioning older people for a new period of service.

PROGRAMS FOR CARING

Church programs for older people tend to fall into the following categories:

- Visitation and conducting worship services and Bible studies in both community and church-sponsored nursing homes.
- Support services for the frail elderly who are still living independently.
- Volunteer telephone visitors, in-home visitors, meals-on-wheels deliverers, transportation providers, and chore service providers.
- Adult day care.
- Support services for caregivers, such as support groups and respite care.

All of these programs use the time and talents of retired church members. What's often missing from these programs, however, is training. Sending out untrained people with instructions just to love the old may be setting them up for failure.

Nursing homes, for example, are frightening places to many people. Everybody has spiritual needs, but those in the nursing home may lack the vocabulary or the means to make their needs known. Volunteers need to be trained to listen for spiritual needs in the areas of meaning, trust, and community among people who may lack a "religious language."

Unfortunately, there is at present no "one-stop shopping" center where a congregation can learn about existing programs for older adults outside its own denomination. A national computerized database would be an ideal solution. A research team from the American Society on Aging's Forum on Religion and Aging is currently at work on a three-volume series of books on ministries with older adults. The second volume of the series will provide a survey of existing programs. However, publication is still years in the future.

INTERGENERATIONAL PROGRAMS

Older people have an enormous spiritual need to remain part of a caring community, giving and receiving love. Intergenerational programs address this need, but church-based interdenominational programs are still few and far between. How do you break down all the artificial barriers and get the generations interacting?

Some examples of intergenerational programs:

Camp Jones Gulch, YMCA Senior Camp in Northern California, is held at the same time as the Y children's camp. Nightly campfires are intergenerational.

Native American elders come to classes with young children in Isleta, New Mexico. They prepare traditional Indian foods, share simple exercises accompanied by native music, sing old songs, and in general help keep their culture alive.

Family Friends, a project of the National Council on the Aging, Inc., trains senior volunteers to help the families of chronically ill children by giving the child individual attention and the parents time off. Teamwork, another NCOA project, trains older people as job coaches for young people with disabilities.

The Elvirita Lewis Foundation in California has pioneered in the training of low-income seniors to work in intergenerational child care centers. These programs raise the income level of retirees and give young children a better quality of care.

All of these models could be used by churches within their own congregations. Churches today, like the rest of society, have single-parent families, divorced people, and hurting children. With their biblical mandate to care for "the widow" and "the fatherless," they should be supporting and nurturing these young families. Who has more time or is better equipped to do it than the grandparents' generation?

DO YOUR OWN SEARCHING

One thing I can almost guarantee is that at retirement nobody is going to take you by the hand and lead you to something that will be a meaningful, joyful use of your time. You're going to have to do your own searching. But there are many opportunities out there. Volunteering is not some kind of lesser calling. If anything, not having to work for money frees you up to do precisely what you want to do, the way you want to do it.

QUESTIONS FOR DISCUSSION

1. What skill or skills would you like to keep using?
2. How can you find out about volunteer opportunities in your community?
3. Do you have any secret interest (such as acting, singing, or sports) that you haven't thought about for years? Is there any way for you to get involved as a volunteer?

CHAPTER SIX

EDUCATION AND TRAVEL ARE WASTED ON THE YOUNG

For every man the world is as fresh as it was the first day,
and as full of untold novelties for him
who has the eyes to see them.
Thomas Huxley

A generation ago, school was for the young only. Today, that has changed drastically. Over a million senior adults are enrolled in degree programs in American colleges and universities. They make excellent students. They're not distracted by youth's need to discover the meaning of life or the desire to party. They're there because they're eager to learn—and teachers love them!

Usually, senior students pull most of the A's in their classes. Behavioral scientists now know that mental ability peaks in the fifties, not the twenties. A person's chronological age and experience are an advantage.

But why would a retiree want to be back in school? Some are pursuing a dream of at last getting the education they could not afford when they were younger. Others are pursuing a career that their parents would not let them have. In the past, parents did not educate girls because "they're going to get married—it would only be wasted." Or parents disapproved of "unsuitable" career choices. Marilyn Maine's parents told her to be a secretary; it was "practical." Yes, but she hated it. After a lifetime doing what someone else told her to do, she's at last at age sixty doing what she wants to do: singing. She plans to continue performing and get a degree in music education.

Some retirees plan to use their new knowledge to help others. Arlene Smith Moore, a retiree from the Butterick Co., enrolled in Penn State University for an associate degree in social work, which she plans to use as a volunteer in her community.

Many more seniors are enrolled in non-degree programs. Some are taking courses that will help them earn money to supplement their retirement income. Personal computer courses are very popular with retirees, and are an essential part of many retirees' small home businesses.

But millions of retirees who are taking courses are doing so for sheer enjoyment. Courses in the arts are booming. Writing courses are also popular, especially with women. So are sports. Many communities have teams for older players in softball, bowling, even tennis and running. Older friends of ours rediscovered skiing after retirement by joining the Over the Hill Gang, a group of over-sixty skiers.

LEARNING CAN BE FUN

Education that you take on *voluntarily* because you're pursuing your own interests (and not somebody else's) is different from the mandatory schooling all of us went through in the past. Learning, especially in the company of other alert, interesting people, is fun. And as my friend Liz Marcellin says, "After forty, we all need maintenance, and *fun is maintenance*."

You may have a problem with this concept. Many of us have not allowed ourselves to have fun for years. Perhaps we were raised by parents who overemphasized work. Perhaps we grew up with a concept of a God who constantly says "No!"

What have you been postponing? If the parental voice inside your head says you can't, ask God. Your heavenly Father loves to say yes to things that are positive, things that will stretch your creativity. He says you can.

SCHOOLS AND COLLEGES WANT YOU!

Colleges and universities in the United States and Canada are actively encouraging adult enrollment. The pool of young adult students is shrinking and universities have to seek new students. So they are reducing their fees and setting up special programs for older adults in order to attract retirees. At least eighteen states waive tuition fees for older students at publicly supported institutions. Eligibility starts at either fifty-five or sixty-five, depending on the state. Other state schools and private schools offer reduced fees for seniors. Inquire at your local college or university about fees and about whether the school offers special programs for seniors.

If you are confined to your home by illness or family responsibilities, or if a college or university is beyond commuting distance, ask if they have an external degree program. These programs enable you to work independently at home, by correspondence, going to campus intermittently to meet with advisors.

The Center for Creative Retirement at the University of North Carolina at Asheville offers College for Seniors, taught by the university faculty. The Center's SAIL program (Senior Academy for Intergenerational Learning) matches retirees as mentors together with college students who are interested in entering their vocations. It then puts the pair to work on a real-life problem. For example, a computer science major and a retired engineer are working together on computerizing a list of resource people for the Center.

COMBINING EDUCATION AND TRAVEL

Learning while traveling is such a hit with seniors that Elderhostel, the largest nonprofit agency devoted to educational travel, grew from a handful of programs in 1975 to hundreds of programs in every U.S. state, Canada, and twenty-seven other countries. In 1989, close to 200,000 people over sixty took part.

Elderhostel programs are sponsored by colleges, universities, church camps and conferences, private foundations, national and state parks, and other educational institutions. Accommodations are in college dormitories, church camp facilities, or modest motels or hotels. There are no exams or grades, but the teachers are all experts in their fields, and the prices are a bargain. One-week programs within the U.S., including tuition and all meals but not including transportation, are usually under $300 per person. Scholarships are available for those who can't afford the fees.

THE SKY'S THE LIMIT!

There is literally something for every interest. The offerings include such choices as gold mining in Alaska; desert ecology in Palm Springs, California; Western history in Montana; jazz at a performing arts institute near Monterey; folk arts in Appalachia; cave geology at Carlsbad Caverns in New Mexico; volcanology at a live, erupting volcano in Hawaii; and much, much more. If you've always wanted to sing, act, weave, paint, or draw, there's an Elderhostel that offers these choices.

International Elderhostel programs cost more, but they offer the same variety of exciting choices. Some include staying in people's homes so that you can meet the natives of the host country.

I had heard so many good things about Elderhostels from friends who'd gone that I couldn't wait until my husband was old enough to qualify. (At least one spouse must be sixty or older.) We attended our first Elderhostel at Volcano National Park in Hawaii last year. It was everything they said it was, and more. The instructors were tops. Field trips included being taken to watch the lava flow from an active volcano. It was the thrill of a lifetime.

OTHER EDUCATIONAL TRAVEL OPPORTUNITIES

In addition, there are many, many educational travel programs designed especially for seniors. Some are much higher in creature comforts than Elderhostel and priced to match. For information, consult your local colleges, universities, and museums, or your travel agent. Major museums, such as the Metropolitan Museum of Art in New York and the Smithsonian Institution in Washington, D.C., all sponsor travel programs.

The number of music festivals in the United States and throughout the world is too large to list. Again, travel agents are knowledgeable about these and other special interest travel opportunities, such as the "cooks tours," with demonstrations by master chefs, or "adventure travel" to natural wonders.

A new trend in the travel industry is grandparents-grandchildren joint travel adventures. These are covered in chapter 16.

QUESTIONS FOR DISCUSSION

1. What have you always wanted to learn?
2. Where have you always wanted to go?
3. What is preventing you for doing either right now?

CHAPTER SEVEN

IF YOU NEED PAID EMPLOYMENT

I've been a physician all my adult life – and I really like the idea of being something else.
Dr. O. Carl Simonton

You may find, after working through the financial planning process prior to retirement, that some kind of work is necessary. Or you may find that volunteering doesn't do it for you – you need to work at something for which you will be paid. The only question is: Do you want to be doing what you've been doing all your life or something else?

If you feel no need to change, your own former company may be the best place to start looking for part-time work. A few large companies prefer to fill available openings with their own retirees. Travelers Insurance Company, for instance, has a retiree job bank. Or your own company may agree to contract with you as a part-time consultant or employee to continue what you've been doing.

Another possible option might be to find work in your field through agencies that place temporary workers. In tight economic times, many companies prefer to contract for workers on an "as-needed" basis. This creates many more opportunities for temporary employment agencies, which now increasingly place managers and professionals for short-term employment, as well as office workers and security guards. The Kelly Services "Encore" Program is specifically targeted to people over fifty-five.

One innovative nonprofit program that specializes in workers over fifty-five is Operation ABLE, which began in Chicago and now has offices in Boston, Detroit, Los Angeles, New York, Lincoln, Nebraska, and Little Rock, Arkansas. ABLE promotes opportunities for older workers through a network of private and public employers, and also counsels, trains, and places job seekers.

Don't overlook local sources of help. Your local Area Agency on Aging may have a "jobs for seniors" program that acts as a nonprofit employment agency. Also, your local community college or university may have free vocational testing, counseling, and job search assistance.

RETIREES AND WORK

According to the Commonwealth Fund in New York:

- One-third of all career jobs end at age fifty-five.
- One-half of all career jobs end at age sixty.
- Nearly two million workers aged fifty to sixty-four are eager to get back into the work force.

Do most retirees want some kind of work? In one survey conducted by a large electronics company, 68 percent of the company's retirees who responded said they did. But few said they wanted to come back to a full forty-hour work week.

According to the U.S. Bureau of Labor Statistics:

- 6 percent of retirees want to work full time.
- 16 percent prefer to work a few hours each day.
- 23 percent prefer to work weeks on and off.
- 55 percent prefer two to three days per week.

Modern Maturity magazine asked its readers if they wanted to work after retirement. The vast majority of over 4,000 people who took the trouble to send in the survey coupon wanted to work, but few wanted to work full-time or continue with their old employment. This time around, they said, they wanted a job that "adds zest to your life . . . takes you places you want to be, or puts new people into your life," even if it would be a step down in status.

Many retirees set themselves up as consultants, billing for their services on an hourly basis instead of receiving a salary. As consultants, they can also set their own hours and decide how much work they want to accept. This really amounts to running a small business, and you may be eligible for some of the small business helps listed in this chapter.

But if you decide, like Dr. Simonton, that it's time to do something different, then the same suggestions given in chapter 4 for assessing your skills and interests would also apply here. By following this process, Alice, a former teacher and curriculum specialist who didn't want to be a teacher anymore, found that her background was perfect for a two-day-per-week job selling educational toys and teaching aids in a small shop where she could be an advisor-consultant to her customers.

SHOULD YOU START A BUSINESS?

Sometimes retirees think that now's the time to make a lifelong dream of owning their own business come true. Colonel Sanders, who started Kentucky Fried Chicken during his retirement years, is frequently held up as an example for others. But the advice of business experts is "Go slow," especially if a business will require the investment of a large sum of money, such as a retirement lump sum pension. A small bed-and-breakfast business in your own home makes sense; a "dream business," such as a country inn requiring a large capital investment, probably does not.

You always hear about the small business success stories, but seldom do you hear about the five out of ten new businesses that fail within the first year. Before you take the plunge and put your future financial security at risk, seek out the free counseling services of the Service Corps of Retired Executives (SCORE), a service of the U.S. Small Business Administration.

A small home business that requires little cash up front is ideal for many retirees. If you want to increase your skills in order to turn a hobby into a business, you can find the courses you need in many community colleges and trade schools. Many people have made that progression in the areas of horticulture, arts and crafts, cooking and baking, clothing design, interior design, and more.

Computer courses can also help you get started on a small

home business. Working with a computer, you can establish your own secretarial or bookkeeping service, desktop publishing, mailing service, travel agency, financial and business consulting service, or library research service. With the right software and some training, retirees can remake almost any vocational skill into a home business. Teachers can tutor at home using educational software; registered dieticians can use programs that analyze the nutritional contents of food and devise special diets; there are even weavers who compose new patterns with the aid of computer graphics programs.

FROM HOBBY TO VOCATION

Can you turn your hobby into a new vocation? That's what Bernice Condit and her late husband, Dan, did. Their twin interests in travel and photography became first a mission, then a small business.

In 1970, after Dan had retired from his career as a research chemist, some doctor friends invited them to spend the summer in the mountains of Afghanistan as part of their Medical Assistance Program team. Dan was the team photographer and Bernice took over the kitchen. But Dan was too busy with color photography to take black and white photos, so he handed Bernice, who had never taken pictures, his camera loaded with black and white film and said, "Here, you do it." When they returned, Dan made copies of his slides and developed Bernice's film in their home darkroom.

The demand for their pictures surprised them. After word got out, they were contacted by additional missions groups, and so they made more trips. Bernice began to develop her own style, specializing in sensitive portraits, especially of women and children. She was becoming an artist, with the camera as her instrument. Their joint adventure in mission photography lasted twenty years, but was suddenly ended when Dan died.

In recent years, their large stock of photos has been in demand by publishers. Bernice now runs a separate for-profit business, Condit Photo Resources, a stock photo agency. In 1983, an exhibit of Bernice's black and white prints entitled "God's Family" was displayed at the Billy Graham Museum on the campus of Wheaton College in Illinois. On an exhibit poster were these words from Bernice:

> The Lord said to Moses, "What is that in your hand?" Moses had a shepherd's staff. Dan and I have each had a camera, which we had been using for personal enjoyment. It is fascinating for us to look back now and see how the Lord was preparing us to use our cameras in His service.

When you perfect your art, take a course for sheer enjoyment, or gain more knowledge just for the love of it, you never know where it might lead. Sometimes it leads to a new and totally unexpected source of income. Older people used to think, "What's the use of trying something new at my age? I'll never use it." They are often wrong.

QUESTION FOR DISCUSSION

1. Have you thought of going back to work? What would you like to do?

CHAPTER EIGHT

WHERE WILL YOU SPEND YOUR TIME?

How does the place feel?
Does it remind us of times
when we've been happy?
Carol Pierskalla, *Rehearsal for Retirement*

So often, people choose retirement lifestyles, even moving considerable distances, without giving any thought to their psychological and emotional needs, much less to what they want to do once they get there.

In his autobiography, *Returning,* Dan Wakefield writes of being addicted in midlife to alcohol and cocaine. One day, almost out of the blue, he came to believe that he would die if he didn't leave Southern California immediately. He returned, not to his boyhood home in the Midwest but to the Beacon Hill neighborhood in Boston where he had felt most at home as a young man. This "returning" was the first step on his spiritual journey back to health and wholeness.

Wakefield's experience is a reminder that places either nurture us or they don't. I grew up in New York City but I never really felt at home there. The Southern Appalachian mountains give me a feeling of welcome. The High Sierras do not.

Trust me, these feelings are real, and you need to heed them. Advertising lures retirees to Sunbelt communities. Some people love them. For others, these moves are a disaster. If you like the stimulation and beauty of the changing seasons, you may be miserable in Florida. If a green setting and rain make you happy, you may hate the Arizona desert. A setting that's enjoyable as a needed change for a two-week vacation will not necessarily nurture you for the rest of your life. It would be much better to realize this *before* you sell your home and invest in a "dream home" in a distant state. You can't live in somebody else's dream.

DOES RELOCATION SUCCEED?

- Nine out of ten people over sixty-five stay where they are.
- One out of thirty moves to an apartment, condo, or smaller home in the same city.
- One in eighty-six moves to another part of the same state, perhaps to a former vacation home.
- Only one in 123 moves to another state. Still, each year, one-quarter of a million people over sixty-five relocate to another state.
- Does relocation succeed? Not always. A University of Miami study in the late 1970s showed that a surprising number of older adults who moved to another state later either moved to still another state or returned home within ten years.[1]

THE FANTASY OF ETERNAL YOUTH

Some retirement communities are sold to older people as fountains of "eternal youth." Residents of a retirement community in Sonoma, California, believe they live in an adults-only paradise. But age discrimination in rental housing is illegal in California unless the adults-only communities meet the "special or physical needs of the elderly."

This puts owners in a bind: Either they rent to families with children, or they have to install curb cuts for wheelchairs and grab bars in bathrooms, and have twenty-four-hour paramedics on call. Residents object to those physical adaptations for the handicapped because, they say, they want to avoid "the depressing atmosphere of a nursing home." To be forced to adopt that kind of an environment, residents say, would interfere with their rights as "active people who are enjoying their lives in retirement, *where they choose not to be old.*"[2]

What? Nobody in this retirement paradise is ever sick? Nobody ever dies? What probably happens is that people who can no longer be active are forced to move away, lest the sight of a frail or ill older person upsets one of the healthy, active "non-old" seniors.

It's dangerous to buy into the fantasy that you can choose not be old. You never know how many years of good health you're going to enjoy. You could end up on the outside looking in when there's no room in "paradise" for human infirmities.

THINK BEYOND THE IMMEDIATE PRESENT

Housing that's right for the active, early years of retirement may not suit the needs of more advanced years, and retirees may be forced to move more than once. Before you make a decision either to stay or to move, ask yourself the following questions:

- If I could no longer shop or cook or clean my home, would I be able to stay in this community? Could I hire help to come in or move to retirement housing in the same community that has these services?
- What will I do in the future if I can no longer drive?
- If I become widowed, can I continue to live here alone?
- Are there medical facilities if I need them?

John had to leave my seminar in St. Petersburg, Florida, early in order to take his parents to the hospital at Florida State University. Although they'd researched a retirement home thoroughly, his parents had given no thought to becoming ill and frail. When they needed specialized medical attention but could no longer drive, John had to drive from St. Petersburg to DeFuniak Springs to pick them up and from DeFuniak Springs to Tallahassee. The one-way trip took him all day. If these elderly parents didn't have John, they would have no way of getting to their doctors' appointments. Needless to say, John has no plans to move out in the boondocks when he retires.

It would be a good idea to visit the Area Agency on Aging, or the Commission on Aging, in any new community you're thinking of moving to (as well as your present community) to find out what services are available to seniors. After you list the pros and the cons for both moving and staying, you'll have a better idea whether you would be gaining or losing by moving.

WILL YOU BLOOM IF YOU'RE TRANSPLANTED?

Moving out of your home community is not a step that should be taken lightly. For many people, beautiful scenery and good weather may not be an adequate substitute for established roots in a community.

In New York, Phil was an advertising executive with a wide circle of friends. He had a reputation not only in his profession but in his community, where he'd been instrumental in raising funds for many civic groups. In Florida, nobody knows — or cares — who Phil was. Every human contact he makes now has to start off from scratch.

Or take a simple, everyday occurrence like being called by name by the local pharmacist who owns the drugstore and knew your parents and also knows your children. In a small town, this is still possible. But at the chain drugstore in a retirement community, the hired pharmacist is a kid just out of school who doesn't know you from Adam. This is more significant than you may realize.

We are invisibly supported by the familiar people and details of everyday life. When these ties are cut, we suffer. Feelings of loneliness, alienation, and depression can overwhelm us. The older you get, the more likely you are to be deeply disturbed by moving. One study of very elderly people who were forced to move out of their home communities compared them to survivors of a natural disaster such as an earthquake. Years later, they were still in shock.

THE IMPORTANCE OF FAMILY

If you think you're an independent creature, able to do everything for yourself, old age will quickly strip away these illusions. If you have a family, someday you will need them. If you live close to them now, do you really want to move so far away that it will become difficult for them to help you? Do you want to lose the ties you have with your grandchildren so that they grow up without you?

Sometimes, retirees wake up years later and realize after it's too late that they did not give enough weight to family relationships after retirement. Dr. Arthur Kornhaber and his wife, Carol, interviewed hundreds of grandparents for the book *Grandparents-Grandchildren: The Vital Connection* by Arthur Kornhaber and Kenneth L. Woodward. This is what they found:

> Seventy percent of the interview subjects who had moved away said that they would not do it over again if they had a choice. They felt out of touch with the emotional life of

> their families. . . . Many were very emphatic about having gone along with the crowd, not thinking about all the implications of what they were doing; looking forward to retirement all their lives and finding it a disappointment. The respondents who had moved away were unanimous in saying that they would not advise their children to do the same.[3]

The following comment is by a grandmother living in a Florida retirement community where there are no children:

> "I used to feel important with my grandchildren, teaching them things, playing with them, proud of them, going to school with them. You know, I was a grandmother in my community. It meant something there. The grandchildren were proud of me. They would show me off to their friends . . . . When we retired, I was so bored. I didn't have that job of being a grandparent. When I went away, the kids grew up without me . . . . It's hard for me to say, but I resent my husband a bit for that. But then, he didn't make me go. I should have listened to my heart."[4]

SHOULD YOU MOVE TO BE NEAR FAMILY?

Sometimes, of course, our children and their families do the moving away. Should you move in retirement to be closer to your children? *Sometimes* it works out. I was grateful that my parents followed us when we moved from Georgia to Florida so that my children did not lose their grandparents. But another retired couple I know of moved from Southern California to Nevada when their married son was transferred. After a couple of years, the young family moved again, but my friends could not afford to follow. Now they feel "stuck" in Nevada, which would never have been their choice as a place to retire.

If you do move to be near family, ask yourself, *Is this a place I would choose to live if they weren't here?* Also, have a candid, open discussion with family to make sure that such an arrangement will work comfortably for them, too.

FAMILY IS NOT ENOUGH

Even though your family members are located where you might like to move, family is not enough.

During a three-month sabbatical leave from her work as Director of Aging Today and Tomorrow for the American Baptist Churches, Carol Spargo Pierskalla "tried out" different retirement living choices. One was a move to a small town in Wisconsin. Disguised in a gray wig to make her look older, Carol found a room in an old Victorian house near her married sister. They had not lived in the same town for most of their adult lives. Writing about this experience, Carol comments:

> I joined a club my sister belongs to and was accepted because of her. . . . While this attitude was very gracious, it was also very strange for me. . . . I desperately missed being accepted for myself as separate from my sister. If I had stayed longer, I would have needed to develop my own friendships both for my own self-esteem and to avoid intruding on my sister's relationships. . . . It wasn't fair to expect her to provide for all my relational needs.[5]

Before moving to be closer to a family member, it might be a good idea to ask yourself, *Do I have the skills, will, and energy to build my own network of friends? What can I contribute both to my family and to a new community? Is this a place where I can feel at home so that I won't be tempted to depend on my family for everything?*

This is particularly important for widows thinking about moving to be closer to their adult children. Expecting them to meet all your needs will put a strain on the relationship, and becoming overly dependent on them will lower your own self-esteem.

TRY BEFORE YOU BUY

It's difficult to know in advance if you will be able to adapt happily to new surroundings. It's best to go slowly and try not to burn all your bridges behind you. Rent rather than buy at first until you see if you like a new community. If you're thinking of retiring where you vacation, spend an off-season there. Keep your options open in case your enthusiasm for that dream retirement location doesn't last.

Roger and Anne fell in love with Ashland, Oregon, a lovely little college town. But after they'd been there for a while, Roger realized that he needed to work and began to think about doing some type of consulting. However, all of his established business contacts were in Sacramento, California, where he had worked all his life. So back they went.

IF YOU DECIDE TO MOVE

Relocating involves time, energy, money, and risk. If you do decide to move to a new community after retirement, you need to research the move carefully and really think about what's important to you.

Do the exploration of your own needs suggested in chapter 5. Really think about your interests. Do you need to be near a good library? Do you deeply enjoy the symphony, the opera, or major league sports? You may need to be in or near a major city. What interests do you want to pursue—for example, art, photography, music, bridge, etc.? Are there groups with similar interests in this new community?

Retirement Places Rated, by Richard Boyer and David Savageau, covers 131 cities and towns that are popular with retirees in sixteen regions of the United States. It gives a detailed analysis of these places, rating them in six categories: money matters, climate, personal safety, services, housing, and leisure living. Under services, the authors consider the availability of doctors and hospitals, transportation, and shopping. Leisure living includes not only outdoor recreation but cultural facilities, libraries, and restaurants.

Places with the best climate and the lowest cost of living are often the places with the worst services and cultural facilities. If you are considering relocating, I'd recommend that you get ahold of *Retirement Places Rated* and answer the questions on pages xviii and xix in order to determine your "Preference Profile"—that is, which of the six categories is most important to you. You can also use the categories and the authors' method of analysis to ask the right questions about any place you are considering for relocation that is not in the book. Many questions about the area you are considering can be answered by paying a visit to the city or county zoning board and the planning commission offices, or even by writing a letter of inquiry to the chamber of commerce.

THE INTANGIBLES OF A MOVE

There are some important considerations when you're considering a move that are difficult to quantify. They have to do with the subculture of a new community, whether that "community" is a house in a new neighborhood, a retirement condo, or an assisted living or lifecare facility. Is the way these people live, their interests and values, compatible with your lifestyle?

For example, social drinking is an important part of the lifestyle of some retirement communities. If you don't want to be part of the daily "happy hour," what will you do? Some communities emphasize a shared activity, such as golf or bridge. What if you hate golf or bridge? You'd be miserable.

Do you enjoy living where neighbors talk to each other? Then you'd better not move into a neighborhood of commuters who are never to be seen outside.

How do you find out these things before you move? Easy. You ask. Even if you have to go up and down the street (or up and down the halls of a condo) knocking on doors, ask the current residents what kind of place this is to live in. Observe the streets, recreation and social halls, and lobbies. Are people interacting with each other or are the common areas deserted? Go to your public library and ask to look at U.S. Census information about the census tract you're considering (1990 information is available). It will tell you a lot.

But no amount of information will substitute for your own instincts and feelings about a place. The rest of your life is too much time to spend in a place where you're not happy. There is a place just for you!

QUESTIONS FOR DISCUSSION

1. Do your present home and community meet your needs? Will they in the future if you should become disabled or widowed?
2. Make a list of the qualities you would like in an ideal retirement home. Do the same with an ideal retirement community.
3. If you are married, have your spouse do the same thing, and then compare lists.

CHAPTER NINE

LOOKING TO THE FUTURE

Be it ever so humble, there's no place like home.
J. H. Payne

Most older Americans don't want to move. A survey of over 1500 Americans over age fifty-five, conducted for AARP, found that 86 percent want to live in their present homes and never move. Seventy-six percent live in detached single-family houses, and 62 percent of these homes are paid for.

But 65 percent of those polled expect to need help with outdoor maintenance, 54 percent say they won't be able to do heavy housework alone, 26 percent say they will need help making trips to the grocery store or the doctor, and 14 percent expect to need help with meal preparation.

Remodeling and modifying a home can adapt it to the needs of older people, but the services needed to stay in the home—lawn mowing, snow shoveling, transportation, etc.—have to come from the surrounding community.

Eighty-eight percent of those polled said they never discuss their needs with anyone. This means that the overwhelming majority are doing no planning for their changing housing needs as they age.

NOT PLANNING IS NOT AN OPTION

People who do not plan are sometimes forced out of their homes when they can no longer cope with the maintenance and upkeep.

Don't let that happen to you. If you move into more suitable housing later, it should be because you choose to. The time to plan for some of these "what if's" is early in retirement.

The problem with most people is *denial*. Old age and disabilities happen to other people—never to *me*! Those of us who've helped our parents during their old age know better. (This is the subject of my book *Caring for Your Aging Parents: When Love Is Not Enough*.) Many families either are forced into making painful decisions or else they face no-win dilemmas because the aging parents stubbornly refused to do any advance planning.

WHEN CIRCUMSTANCES TAKE AWAY YOUR HOME

Sometimes people think, "I'll just stay put." But remember that in the next ten to twenty years, your surroundings could change drastically.

Dorothy Erb, a seventy-two-year-old retired librarian, couldn't afford to move out of her deteriorating Oakland, California, neighborhood, so she fought back. She led a Home Alert program that organized the neighbors to report drug dealers to the police, even though the crack dealers torched her car in an effort to silence her. Her courage was an inspiration to the younger families, and together they eventually took their streets back from the criminals who had been controlling them.

Unfortunately, some older people neither move nor fight back. Instead, they spend their last years as prisoners in their own homes, too attached to them to consider moving, and too frightened to go outside. The only way around falling into this trap is to plan for the needs of your later years while you're still strong enough to take action. If you wait until the need arises, it may be too late.

MAKE NEEDED CHANGES

What are some of your options for meeting your housing needs in your later years? Here are some suggestions.

Adapt your present home. Even small changes—for example, adding grab bars, handrails, or seats in the bathtub or shower, and replacing hard-to-grip door handles with levers—may make it possible for you to continue living in your present home. Adding ramps and enlarging doorways to make a home wheelchair accessible will probably require hiring a contractor, but even so, this is almost always cheaper than moving.

If you own your home, you have probably built up enough equity to pay for needed remodeling. A home equity loan or a home equity conversion (also known as a reverse annuity mortgage) through a local bank could enable you to get the cash you need out of your house. The advantage of an home equity loan, or HEC, is that no repayments are due during your lifetime.

In order to avoid accidents, your home will need to be well lit. Older people need two to three times as much wattage to see as people in their twenties. Tactile tools to feel your way and low vision aids help people whose eyesight is failing to remain independent. For the hard of hearing, a number of devices can convert the sound of the telephone, doorbell, or smoke alarm to flashing lights. Telephone adapters and amplifiers are widely available.

A local Area Agency on Aging may be able to provide or recommend someone who can come to your home, assess your needs, and make suggestions.

HOME SHARING ARRANGEMENTS

What if you're widowed? Some people enjoy living alone. But others don't because of precarious health or the need for companionship. What are some options?

Share your home. There are a number of ways you can do this. You could rent out extra bedrooms, or you could add or convert living quarters, which you exchange for services. My widowed friend Lois wanted to add a cottage next to her home to provide housing for college students in exchange for yard and maintenance work around the house. Unfortunately, the city zoning board objected. Finally, she was allowed to add a room, bath, and half-kitchen attached to her present home. The arrangement has worked quite well for her for a number of years.

If you don't want to have students (located through a nearby college or university's housing office) or find your own tenants, the National Shared Housing Resource Center through its local affiliates matches older people with housing to offer to older people seeking a place to live.

Build an "in-law" cottage in an adult child's back yard. Or add an accessory apartment to an adult child's house. Check local zoning laws for the feasibility of this option.

One version of this plan is ECHO housing. ECHO stands for Elder Cottage Housing Opportunity (these are also sometimes called "granny flats"). In some states they are available as manufactured units especially designed for older or disabled persons, which can be installed next to an existing house. Most local governments require special use permits for these units.

RETIREMENT HOUSING OPTIONS

Congregate housing. This is a growing trend in the housing industry. You rent private living quarters and pay a monthly fee, which includes meals in a central dining room, housekeeping and transportation services, and planned activities for the residents. In addition, some congregate housing facilities are beginning to add "assisted living" (help with dressing, supervision of medication and health care, etc.).

Many older people resist moving into these facilities, but at a certain stage in life, congregate housing may offer *more* rather than less freedom than your own home. Pearl, a seventy-nine-year-old widow, did not drive, no longer had the energy to cook or entertain friends, and was fast becoming a shut-in. At her age and in her state of health, "independence" meant loneliness and isolation.

After she moved into congregate housing, she was able to get out into the community frequently in the van and invite people over to dinner in the facility's private dining room. She also stopped worrying about what would happen if she fell.

If you decide on this option, you are usually required to move in while you are still mobile. If your health is too poor, you will not be accepted. Also, some facilities have long waiting lists. You need to think seriously about this long before you are ready to move.

One couple that I know chose this option because the husband was much older than his wife and anticipated that she would be widowed. He felt she would be much better off surrounded by a supportive community of other widows than alone in their former home. It turned out that he was right.

Continuing care, or life care, communities. These communities are similar to congregate care communities, but they charge an entrance fee in addition to monthly fees. Also, they guarantee your care for life, including nursing home care if this should become necessary. This is the most expensive option and the riskiest, for if you don't like it, if the service deteriorates, or if the facility goes bankrupt, your money is gone and you may have nowhere else to go.

Since AARP estimates that over the years one such lifecare plan in ten goes bankrupt or gets into financial difficulties, you should proceed with caution. You will want a lawyer and an accountant to check the contract, the actuarial projections, annual reports, and other documents. A number of free and low-cost booklets are available that will help you know what questions to ask when you look over these facilities.

Residential care facilities. These facilities are also known as "board and care" homes. They are generally less expensive than congregate housing. Each resident gets a room or a shared room plus services rather than a private apartment. The monthly fee covers room, board, utilities, housekeeping, laundry, assistance with personal care and medications, and, in some places, recreation. Some states license these facilities. The best have a "homey" atmosphere with caring people running them, but the quality varies widely.

Nursing homes. These are skilled nursing facilities for people whose doctors order around-the-clock nursing care and who cannot be taken care of any other way. Nursing homes are incredibly expensive. (How to pay for nursing home care is covered in chapter 20 of this book. How to choose a nursing home is covered in chapter 11 of my book *Caring for Your Aging Parents: When Love Is Not Enough.*)

LIVING WITH ADULT CHILDREN

Most older people do not want to live with their adult children. Is this never a good idea? I know of several cases where it's worked out very well. Both of these older people were widows who had a good relationship with their adult daughter and son-in-law. Both were excellent communicators who were very up-front about their feelings and both made a real effort to understand the younger couple's point of view, especially their need for psychological "space."

Each of these older widows had relatively strong financial resources and a large house. The younger couples had less money but more energy to provide the household services. They did the house and yard work and most of the cooking in return for a reduced rent. (However, there can be tax consequences for charging less-than-market-value rent to a relative. Before entering into such an arrangement, see your tax advisor.)

Another widow I know of moved in with her grandchildren, a young working couple with a year-old baby. An energetic sixty-eight-year-old, this widow provided childcare for her great-grandchild in return for room and board. Soon, I heard, she got bored and started doing the cooking, too. ("My daughter and son-in-law think they've died and gone to heaven," the baby's grandmother commented.) Before she moved in, the entire family had a thorough discussion, airing all the possible problems and how they'd handle them. So far, it's been working out beautifully.

Even though living with an adult son or daughter may turn out well, neither generation should just assume that it's "the right thing to do" without giving it a lot of thought and discussion.

Before moving in with an adult child, here are some things to think about:

- Is there anyone in the household you don't get along with? This in itself should serve as a red flag.
- Will you be able to bring any of your own furnishings with you? Your pets, if you have any?
- Will you contribute financially to the household?
- What household chores will you share?
- Can you provide your own transportation?
- Will you have any responsibilities for taking care of the children? Do you have disagreements with the parents over the grandchildren—for example, discipline? (Another red flag!)
- Will you be able to entertain your friends and pursue your own interests?
- Can you talk frankly with your family members about things that bother you? Are they able to listen? Are you able to listen when they bring up things that bother them?
- If you become ill, who will take care of you?

GET RID OF "STUFF"

Erma Bombeck, that great popular philosopher, once wondered in one of her columns what would happen to her possessions after her death. Would anybody else appreciate thirty-five years' worth of "empty boxes and secondhand ribbons, jewelry boxes containing religious medals, bowling pin lamps, candle stubs, broken umbrellas, a fur coat from a prehistoric animal, (children's) spelling papers from grade school"?

The answer is no. To paraphrase Ecclesiastes, there's a time for accumulating things and there's a time for divesting yourself of all that "stuff." Even though, as Bombeck says, for some people to throw something away is like undergoing major surgery without an anesthetic, do it. Don't make your children have to do it for you.

Think of it not as a loss, but a gain. It will unclutter your life. Sometimes choosing to move to a smaller place is a marvelous opportunity both to throw things away and to give away prized possessions so you can enjoy the recipient's pleasure.

On our shelves right now is heirloom china and glassware given to us by my late mother-in-law when she moved into a trailer in Florida. Shortly after she moved, a fire broke out and she lost everything. At the time, I was wondering why she was giving her things away early; now, I'm so glad she did.

GRIEF AND THE LOSS OF A HOME

It's not appropriate to talk about these housing moves as if we were discussing going out and buying a new pair of shoes. We love our homes. We wouldn't be human if we didn't get attached to these places where so many of our memories are lodged. Anytime you decide that it's best to move, whether you're giving up a family home you've lived in most of your life or moving to a retirement home you've picked out with great care, you are going to feel grief, and perhaps even anger. You need to recognize and deal with these feelings, lest they overwhelm you with depression.

What cherished mementos of the house can you take with you when you move? Are there possessions from the house that you can't take that you can give to family members so they'll have something special to help them remember the house?

What can you do to "say goodbye" to the house? Having some ritual, celebration, or party may help you to deal with your inevitable grief. (You may find some valuable suggestions in the book *Praying Our Goodbyes* by Joyce Rupp.)

Your children will also grieve the loss of their childhood home—*even if they haven't lived in it for years.* There may be many good reasons why you have to give up this home—it's too big for you to take care of, it's too expensive, the neighborhood has gone downhill, etc. But for your children, this house that no longer meets your needs was their fixed point of reference. It was the place they always came "home" to for holidays and vacations, the place to which they brought their children.

Sandra, my young friend in her twenties, told me that she and her brothers and sister were upset because their parents were selling their big house and moving into a condo. "Where will we go for Christmas?" her married sister asked. The selling of that home marks the end of an era in that family's history. Before a new era can begin, they will first have to say goodbye to the old.

If you have to move—even though in many ways you and your children would rather you stay—try to be patient during the transition period and allow yourselves time to grieve. Even if are anxious to move, even if you know you *should* move, you will still feel sadness at what must be left behind.

QUESTIONS FOR DISCUSSION

1. Could your present home by adapted for your possible future needs?
2. If you couldn't continue living in your present home, where would you go?
3. Start a discussion (with your spouse, a family member, or a friend) about how you will prepare for the housing needs of advanced old age.

PART THREE

CARING FOR THE IMPORTANT PEOPLE IN YOUR LIFE

CHAPTER TEN

THE POST-RETIREMENT MARRIAGE

I married you for better or for worse,
but not for lunch.
Anonymous

"Life is wonderful since Jack retired," June told me. "We're having fun!"

Finally, for couples who are *friends*, there is time to enjoy each other's company. According to researchers, the happiest times in a marriage are the years before children are born and the later years, after the children have grown up and left the nest.

Why then does the divorce rate rise sharply after retirement?

I used to think that the oft-quoted line, "I married you for better or for worse, but not for lunch," was a joke, but I've since learned differently.

RETIREMENT CAN INCREASE CONFLICT

When life follows a preestablished pattern, there are few decisions to be made. But when a major life change such as retirement comes along, there are surprisingly more decisions, and thus more potential for conflict.

If a couple are eight to ten years apart in age, they may be in different stages of their adult development. He may be longing to let go of work and do something else, while she is just hitting her stride in her career. She may want and need to go on working, but what if he wants them to take off in their RV and become gypsies?

Or relocate to a retirement community?

Couples have more time not only to have fun but also to disagree after retirement. Suddenly they're thrown together twenty-four hours a day, seven days a week. Some marriages endure so many years only because work has kept a couple at a safe distance from each other. Retirement takes this distance away.

Harry was an airline pilot who was away from home a great deal; Margo was a secretary. When they both retired and moved to Florida, Harry had a great many hobbies and outside interests, but Margo had none. Before retirement, he had either been too busy or too absent to notice that he didn't much care for Margo's company. He now spends as much time as he can in his workshop, trying to get away from her.

Margo's neighbors feel sorry for her, but they avoid her, too. Her conversation is silly, irritating, and repetitive. Some of the neighbors have tried to get her interested in some activity outside the home, but without success. Margo is refusing to grow and change, and her husband is tired of her.

Can this post-retirement marriage be saved?

SHARP INCREASE IN LATE-LIFE DIVORCES

According to the National Center for Health Statistics, while divorce in general declined in the United States during the decade from 1981 to 1991, divorce in couples married thirty years or more *increased* sharply. Overall divorce went from 5.3 per 1000 to 4.7 per 1000 during the decade, while divorce in thirty-plus marriages increased 16 percent. The number of divorces among older couples in the year 1970 was 17,000; in 1988, it was 35,000.

A sixty-five-year-old corporate executive, married twenty-four years, said, "Things were bad for years, but we thought of ourselves as a couple. Finally, the kids were grown. It was just the two of us without any buffers, and we just decided it was ridiculous to waste the rest of our lives this way."

Social scientists speculate that as people realize they're going to live longer, they are no longer willing to spend those years in an unhappy marriage.

THE POST-RETIREMENT BLUES

The early post-retirement years can be rough. Retirees may go through a period of grief, mourning their lost work identity and doubting their worth. They may be grouchy, irritable, depressed, lethargic—reactions that are hard to live with, even though they're all part of the adjustment process.

When Bill retired from the Navy, he was in his fifties, still full of enthusiasm and energy, but nothing he tried as a second career seemed to work for him. Nan, his wife, suffered right along with him, but there was little she could do. Bill felt like a failure until someone suggested that he might enjoy teaching. He's now teaching English as a second language to immigrant children in junior high school, and he loves it. Once he found his new purpose in life, the marriage quickly recovered from the trauma caused by retirement.

If your marriage has weathered all the storms of life so far, including the societal changes that began in the sixties, chances are it can also weather retirement. This is just one more challenge for the two of you.

WHAT ARE YOUR EXPECTATIONS?

Sometimes post-retirement marital problems can be caused by unspoken expectations. Traditional husbands who've built their identity on their work may need help and support from their wives while they reinvent their lives. But what exactly do husbands expect? What do wives expect? And how do they communicate their expectations to each other?

Catherine became her husband's "activity director" in retirement, thinking up things to occupy him, and giving up her own interests to be his full-time companion. She felt that he expected it, and she gave in to this. But deep down inside, she began to resent him. Still, they never talked about it.

POWER STRUGGLES AND TURF WARS

When we lived in Florida, I used to see retired couples in the supermarket doing the grocery shopping together. He'd put something in the cart. She'd snatch it back, snapping, "We don't need that." Sometimes a heated argument would break out right in the aisle between the packaged cereal and the canned goods. Such power struggles can be expected whenever two people haven't talked through their differing needs and expectations.

In a traditional marriage, the wife has reigned supreme within their home. But when retirement comes along, all of a sudden she has competition on her home turf.

"I'm going crazy," said one wife, who happens to be five feet tall. Her husband is over six feet. "Paul has rearranged my kitchen shelves so that everything I need is on top, out of my reach!"

No doubt Paul thought he was "helping" by making the kitchen more efficient. But this is not how his wife interpreted it. He'd invaded her space. (Note: "my" kitchen shelves!)

Husbands complain that if they try to help around the house, their efforts are subjected to subtle criticism and putdowns. "Nothing I do comes up to her standards," Don told a counselor. "She grabs the vacuum cleaner out of my hand and does it over."

The message Don is getting from Jane is that he's too stupid and incompetent to be trusted to do the simplest task around the house. He feels that he's being attacked, and he also feels diminished and hurt by what he perceives as her contempt.

WHAT'S THE SOLUTION?

"How is a couple going to divide up the time and turf when they're together in the same house twenty-four hours per day? This is something that has to be consciously thought out and not just something they fall into," says Kenneth W. Fors, who has done pre-retirement counseling for over twenty-five years. He recommends that couples take a pre-retirement class together, and that they enter retirement as a team. Try to anticipate what retirement might be like. Really talk about it.

Certain questions must be discussed. Will the retiring spouse take over any of the household chores? If so, which ones? When?

An exercise Fors uses that you might find helpful is for each of you to fill out a schedule called "a typical day in retirement," which covers the complete daily routine from getting up in the morning to going to bed at night. Then compare notes. If your projections are similar, all well and good. If not, you need to work out your differences.

When one person is retired and the spouse is not, their daily schedules may be out of sync. Trudy, a dental hygienist, used to resent the fact that Mac was still sleeping when she got up to go to work and he sometimes spent the day playing golf, and the fact that he even put off doing chores around the house.

"It took me about a year to adjust to the change," Trudy said.

"It still gets on my nerves a little, but I've got to allow him to be retired even if I'm not."

Why do so many couples attack each other instead of their problems?

HIDDEN ANGER AND FEAR

"There's a lot of hidden anger in some older women," says Priscilla Tudor, who counsels older individuals and couples, and facilitates a support group for people over sixty-five. "They may have derived all their self-worth from their roles as wife and mother without ever being recognized for what they were contributing. The wife feels she's never got much out of this marriage all those years. Now he's making new demands on her, and she's angry."

Husbands may also be angry over the loss of their careers without being willing or able to talk about it. They may feel inadequate. Both husbands and wives may fear financial insecurity, or fear for their future health. Yet they never admit their fears to each other. With all of these unresolved feelings bubbling below the surface, it's no wonder that post-retirement marriages sometimes blow up.

What's the answer? Talk to each other about your feelings, says Christian marriage counselor Robert Richards, Ph.D.

"The more you talk about it, the better," he says. "Couples who just plunge into it—it's retirement time—whoopee!—can have some very bad things happen."

BEING WILLING TO SHARE

But power struggles are not inevitable.

Students of human behavior say that as men and women age, they often develop neglected areas of their personalities. Men may become more nurturing and take more interest in the family and domestic details; women may take more interest in finances, a job outside the home, and outside affairs in general.

Marital partners who don't feel threatened by these changes can benefit from them. Marilyn continued to teach for three years after her husband's retirement. Steve learned to cook and shop, and took pride in his newfound skills. When Charlie, a semi-retired executive, started getting interested in doing more cooking, his wife, Peg, didn't fight it. She moved over and shared what had been her territory, letting him have some of what he wanted in the kitchen.

ONE EYE ON THE FUTURE

With her husband's full approval, Karen is training herself to travel alone. "If I'm widowed," she says, "I don't want to become one of these women who refuse to go anywhere because their husbands always took care of travel arrangements."

It makes sense to look ahead. In the future, one of the marital partners may become too ill to do his or her usual "jobs" in the marriage, and one of them will almost surely spend some time widowed. Both need to be cross-trained in the other's area of expertise in order to survive.

Anna is a lady in her seventies who broke her arm and a rib, and had to be hospitalized. George, her husband, had never learned to fix himself a meal. Fortunately, members of their church were happy to help by bringing in casseroles, but the ladies couldn't help wondering why, in this day and age, this healthy, mentally competent man couldn't even operate a microwave.

George had been raised to believe that men weren't supposed to be able to cook and Anna had been raised to believe that it was her job to feed him. The same thing happens in reverse when women take no interest in financial matters because that's their husband's job. Then they're widowed and they don't even know how to balance a checkbook. They can become easy prey for financial sharks and lose everything.

Life is unpredictable. Neither partner can know when one of them might have to take over for the other. The early years of retirement are an excellent time to begin learning.

RENEGOTIATE YOUR MARRIAGE

So many areas of life are bound to change for a retiring couple. It's almost like negotiating marriage anew. For example, here are some things you need to think about:

Togetherness. How much "space" does each partner want and need? John and Helen do almost everything together in retirement. Each morning, they sit down and plan their day. Both of them like it this way, but Ralph and Judy would feel suffocated if they had to live like this. Both maintain separate daily schedules, but plan activities they enjoy doing together on a weekly basis. What kind of pattern do you want to follow in retirement? Do you each allow the other to have individual friends in addition to your mutual friends? Will you continue to enjoy your own unique interests and talents?

Most retirement marriages, counselors believe, would benefit from giving each other *more* space rather than less. If you're always together, neither of you will have anything fresh to talk to the other about.

"Personal contentment is very important in helping a marriage relationship," Dr. Richards says. "Two people who have learned to get fulfillment and to get their needs met in other parts of their life as well as from each other feel content with themselves. The marriage benefits from it."

Sex. Will your sex lives change as the result of having more time for each other? Will one partner make more demands on the other? Does one partner feel bored and want to spice things up? Does one partner want more romance than the other? Does one or both feel upset by the normal slowing down of responses due to aging?

Intimacy. How much of yourself have you been willing to reveal to your partner? Do each of you want to know each other more deeply, or are you looking for more intimacy while your partner is not?

Money. Unfortunately money is another big area of potential conflict. How will you handle a reduced income? How much will you spend and save? What investments will you make? Cutting back on spending after retirement can lead to some lifestyle changes—a decision to move where housing will be cheaper, for instance—that have a big impact on a marriage.

Even economizing by cutting back to one car instead of two might lead to unhappiness and conflict. Does one spouse go everywhere with the other because there's only one car? If so, neither one of them is being allowed enough space. Is one spouse forced to give up activities and stay home because the other needs the car?

Family concerns. How can you know what kind of caregiving help may be needed by an elderly parent? (See chapter 6 of my book *Caring for Your Aging Parents* for suggestions on preserving your marriage while helping your parents.) How much help will you need or want to give your adult children? How often do you want to see them? If this is a second marriage for you and your spouse, there may be two sets of children to talk about. If you have or expect to have grandchildren, what kind of grandparents do you want to be?

Health. Are you both willing to take responsibility for making some of the lifestyle changes needed to preserve your health as you age? In most traditional marriages, the wife tends to take responsibility for her husband's health, shopping for and preparing the food, nagging him to get more exercise, and so on. But if anything happens to her, he may have been made unable to take care of himself. Both need to learn intelligent self-care and to encourage each other to practice it.

Faith. Are you able to talk to each other openly about your beliefs and to encourage each other's spiritual growth? This is very important as you age.

The person who wants to age successfully needs to change his entire value system, according to researcher Margaret Clark. If, like so many men and women in our society, you have valued status and achievement, then you need to learn to value congeniality and to desire to be loved, not feared. If you fear and mistrust others, that means you have to learn to depend on them. Or, if you have been one to value control all your life, you need to learn to give up trying to control the external world and learn to control your own inner reactions.

If you have always tended to be ambitious and competitive, then you need to learn to become relaxed and cooperative. And if throughout your life you have tried to acquire more things, you now need to learn to conserve what you have. You must substitute new goals for the old ones that are no longer possible. "It seems likely that patterns of value appropriate to the middle-aged in our society are deemed inappropriate (or prove dysfunctional) for the elderly," says Dr. Clark.[1]

All of these "values"—love, trust, control, dependence, etc.—are spiritual issues, or issues of faith. You can't *make* anybody else change, even for his or her own good, but you can work on your own faith, and you can encourage your spouse to do the same.

POSITIVE STEPS YOU CAN TAKE

Working together on some of the "Questions for Discussion" at the end of the chapters in this book may open up communication on some issues that you might never otherwise think of discussing. It's unlikely, if you both regard your marriage as happy, that you've come this far without developing communication and problem-solving skills. But there is always room for improvement.

A program with the goal of making good marriages better is Marriage Encounter. It helps you learn how to affirm each other by focusing on the positive qualities that attracted you to this partner in the first place.

Paul Fremont Brown and his wife, Alice, were in their early fifties when they tried a Marriage Encounter weekend retreat. In his book *From Here to Retirement,* Fremont reports, "In this short weekend, we discovered more about ourselves and our relationship than we had learned in our previous thirty years of marriage."[2]

FIND NEW THINGS TO DO TOGETHER

Sometimes couples have led parallel lives. Most of their interests are somewhat similar but separate ones. Retirement is the perfect time to try something new. Why not look for something you will both enjoy doing together?

Tom and Lil decided they needed more exercise. They joined a seniors group that goes "mall walking" every morning. Ralph and Anne started playing golf together. Ralph was a duffer and Anne had never tried it, but they're learning together. Joe and Marilyn became collectors and "antique hounds." They enjoy spending time looking near home and when they travel, and learning more about the objects they've been collecting. Helen and Ralph, who had always taught separately, began "team teaching" a Sunday school class.

Another approach to joining together in some of your activities is for one partner to introduce the other to an interest that has long been part of his or her life. When Dan took Marge on his rockhound expeditions in the mountains, she became fascinated. "Why didn't I ever do this before?" she wondered.

Charlie told Peg he wanted her to go to baseball games with him. After retirement, he planned to follow his team to some of their out-of-town games. So she agreed. "But," she said, "if I go to baseball games with you, I want you to have afternoon tea with me." So after every game, they scout out a shop or hotel that serves an elegant afternoon tea. What began as an almost grudging, tit-for-tat exchange has become a source of real pleasure to both of them. Think of it as life enrichment.

ALLOW CHANGES TO TAKE PLACE

In their marriage, Jim had always initiated joint activities, vacations, etc. But after retirement, he was tired of the weight of responsibility. So he told Sally, "I want you to do some initiating, too." Sally agreed, and their marriage has benefited immensely.

We all have different ways of showing love that we learned from our families when we were growing up. But it may not be what feels like love to your mate. You can encourage your spouse to ask for the changes he or she wants by saying, "What do I do that makes you feel really loved?"

When Tim Hansel, a Christian author and speaker tried that, he was sure his wife would say, "When you bring me flowers, I feel really loved," because that's something he frequently did. But her answer surprised him. She said, "When you're on time!" That really hit him. It never occurred to Tim that his habitual lateness made his marriage partner feel uncared for. After that, he made more of an effort to be prompt.

Ethel knew her marriage was changing by the way Hank reacted when their daughter and her family moved overseas as missionaries. He surprised her by crying for two days. "If he hadn't done that, I would have felt even worse," Ethel said. She would have had to express grief for both of them.

Many women have been in charge of the emotional dimension for the entire length of the marriage. The balance in Ethel's marriage is now shifting. She didn't ask for this change, but wisely, she's allowing it to happen.

If you can allow your marriage to change, I have good news. As one of my friends said about her marriage of forty years, "It keeps getting better." But you both have to work at it.

SEEK HELP

If you and your mate can't talk to each other about some of the issues in this chapter, or if you've tried but can't resolve the problems, will counseling help? Or is it too late to change?

No, it's not too late, says marriage counselor Robert Richards. "I'm continually impressed by how much change older people can make. 'You can't teach an old dog new tricks' is not true. The success of counseling really depends on the willingness of couples to stay in the process and see it through for however long it takes, not their age."

While some older people aren't willing to do this, those who are willing can be helped.

QUESTIONS FOR DISCUSSION

1. What would you like to see changed in your marriage after retirement?
2. Are there any new activities you'd like to try doing together as a couple?

CHAPTER ELEVEN

WHEN YOU BECOME THE SURVIVING SPOUSE

When you lose a spouse, you feel like half a person.
You have to work to become a whole person again.
Betty Coe, Founder, Christian Widowed Fellowship

After she was widowed, my mother-in-law said something I will never forget: "Everybody enters this world and leaves it alone." Even if we start retirement as part of a married couple, sooner or later, one of us will die and the survivor will be alone.

This is not pleasant to think about, but think about it we must. Not only is protecting the survivor an important goal of financial planning, but protecting the survivor psychologically and emotionally (insofar as this is possible) should be an important part of retirement planning in general.

Is there anything that can be done to cushion the blow or help the survivor recover more easily from this excruciatingly painful experience? What can we learn from those who've gone before us?

FINDING SOMEONE WHO UNDERSTANDS

It's almost impossible, widows and widowers say, for those who have not experienced this loss to understand what a person is going through. This was Betty Coe's experience. Her husband died suddenly at age sixty-three just before their fortieth wedding anniversary. "Luckily," she said, "God puts us in shock. Otherwise, we could never stand it."

In shock, grief-stricken people, feeling "this can't be true!" go through the motions of living—dazed, scarcely aware of their surroundings, unable to concentrate, unable to think clearly. That's why the widowed are advised to make no major decisions about the course of their future, especially such things as moving or remarriage, for at least a year.

Sleeplessness is part of the process. The doctor gave Betty medication, but it did no good. He took her off it, saying, "You'll simply have to tough it out." Well-meaning people told her that her husband was "in heaven," and "with God right now."

"I knew that," Betty said, "but it did not help. I still have the feeling, although I know otherwise in my mind, that it's not true."

"One of the first things I did," Betty continues, "was to get down on my knees and ask forgiveness for the many times in the past that I'd said similar things to other people. I just didn't *know*!"

The grieving process took her two years. Although the length of grieving is different for each person, two years is not unusual for this most severe initial period.

MISTAKES THE WIDOWED MAKE

Betty made the very common mistake of moving too soon. She'd been living with her husband in Michigan and working as an apartment manager. After her husband's death, she moved to California since six of her seven children lived there, staying with each of them in turn. But being taken away from her normal contact with people in her job, together with suddenly not having a home of her own, delayed her recovery.

"All this moving around—I was just running away. But you can't run away," Betty said. One year after her husband's death, her depression was so deep, "Without the Lord, I'd have just walked off a bridge. I kept praying, but there were no answers."

Then she saw a newspaper story about Widowed Persons Services of AARP run by Ruth Nevin. "I said, 'Lord, that's not for me!' Then the Lord showed it to me a second time, but I kept resisting. Like a lot of people, I clung to the verse, 'I can do everything through him who gives me strength,' but I forgot that God often works through *people*. The third time, I called the number. The lady who answered said she'd send somebody out to talk to me."

Others had told Betty that she'd just have to get over it. But the widow who came in response to her phone call told her that she wouldn't get over it. She'd have to learn to cope with it. Betty learned that her whole life had to change. She had to accept the fact that her husband was gone. She had to accept the fact that she was alone and she had to rebuild a life for herself as a single person.

FINDING HOPE AGAIN

To help her do this, Betty took an eight-week course given by Ruth Nevin under the sponsorship of Widowed Persons Service. She was also invited to attend a play with a group of widows. These women had gone through what she had, but they were so jolly. Betty began to hope that if they could do it, she could, too.

"During the time I was taking these classes, the deep-down hurt left me and God put peace in my heart," Betty said. After she began to heal she took the WPS training in order to become a peer counselor for others.

What happens in these groups that makes such a difference? "Putting into words the actual experience with the dying loved one results in a release taking place and creates a bond with others in the group," says Ruth Nevin, who has worked with widowed groups for over fourteen years. A retired high school guidance counselor, she began working with a widowed support group at her church that later became a branch of the nationwide Widowed Persons Service of AARP.

GRIEVING IS A PROCESS

Ruth also trains the Widowed Persons Service's peer counselors. Referrals to WPS come from pastors, doctors, singles groups, hospices, and friends who are in contact with the grieving. Widowed people can pour out their hearts to these peer counselors, who will stay with them in the process for as long as it takes. Ruth and the people who work with the widowed through WPS are all volunteers who've been widowed themselves and understand because they've been there.

"I'm a great hugger," Ruth said. "This is so important. The first thing that you miss when you lose a spouse is the touching.

My hugs say, 'I've been there. I understand. I care.' To watch the pain disappear from people's eyes—to watch them come back to life—that's my reward."

Most people do not realize that grieving is *work*, and that until you go through this process—do the work—you can't get on with your life. Being "stuck" in any stage of the grief process, whether it's shock, denial, anger, or blame, can lead to a life-threatening depression.

Fortunately, grief counseling is becoming more widely available, whether through private counselors, or at little or no cost through hospital chaplain services, or hospice services, to bereaved families. Instead of suffering in silence, you can get help for yourself or for someone you know who is grieving.

CAREGIVING AS A PREPARATION

Betty Coe's widowhood was as sudden as a clap of thunder, but many widows and widowers experience the death of a spouse as a long, slow process. When that happens, much of the caregiver's grieving occurs while the loved one is still alive.

The marriage relationship changes drastically when one partner becomes ill, and thus dependent on the other. The dependent partner may be angry and resentful, having lost his or her role in the marriage. And the caregiving partner also may be angry and sad, having lost the nurturing and aid that he or she was used to receiving.

In addition to the physical care of a spouse, the caregiver has to take on all of the usual responsibilities in the marriage as well. Like most widows, the caregiving wife usually seems to have the most difficulty with the financial management and decision-making aspects of life her husband formerly took care of. Like most widowers, the caregiving husband has the most difficulty with household management—the cooking, cleaning, and laundry that his wife formerly handled.

"In some ways, it's worse than widowhood," one caregiver commented. "You've lost your husband, even though he's still alive. Nobody understands what it's like to be married, yet not married."

Loneliness is a given for caregivers. The ill spouse is no longer able to participate in activities they used to enjoy together as a couple, nor is the well spouse free to participate in most social activities. Frequently caregivers become isolated from former friends, and even from family.

"I couldn't talk to my children," said Mary, a wife whose husband was in a nursing home after she could no longer care for him at home. "I thought I was just explaining things to them, but they said I was complaining about their father."

CAREGIVERS AT RISK

Overwhelming grief, anger, and guilt are typical emotions of caregivers, together with physical exhaustion. Everybody tends to focus on the patient, but the caregiver is also at risk.

In 1990 the Family Survival Project in San Francisco published the results of a yearlong study of 1337 caregivers of brain-impaired adults in California. The caregivers, whose average age was sixty-one, were 75 percent female. Fully 68 percent showed symptoms of clinical depression. Caregivers in the lowest income range were older, in worse physical and mental health, and experienced more patient problem behaviors.

Caregivers tend to get so caught up in their role that they ignore their own needs. They think that's the only loving thing to do. But as Dr. Dean Ornish, a well-known cardiologist, says, "The heart has to pump blood to itself first." And nobody has ever accused the heart of selfishness. Unless caregivers learn to take care of their own needs, they will burn out.

Unfortunately, the marital partner receiving care may become so dependent that he doesn't want to let the caregiver out of his sight. Or the caregiving partner may come to believe, "Nobody else can do this job like I can. As long as I'm here, nothing bad can happen." It's a way of maintaining control.

But sometimes, the outcome is tragic.

GET HELP BEFORE IT'S TOO LATE

"Rossmoor Murder-Suicide Ends Couple's Battle with Alzheimer's," was a recent newspaper headline. August Spamer, described by neighbors as a beautiful and kind eighty-five-year-old gentleman, shot and killed his wife of sixty-five years before pulling the trigger on himself. Lotte Spamer, eighty, suffered from Alzheimer's disease, and her husband, distressed at the prospect of placing her in a nursing home, chose death for both of them over separation.

"He didn't do it because he hated her. He did it because

he loved her," a neighbor was quoted as saying. "People are so funny. They won't ask for help."

It's possible that August Spamer killed his wife out of "love." But it's more likely that he was in such a state of physical exhaustion and depression that he went over the edge. Alzheimer's patients can keep you up day and night. Try going without sleep for three or four nights. It makes you crazy.

A great deal of help, such as support groups and respite care, is available for Alzheimer's victims and their families in many communities. But nobody can force you to accept help even if it's available. People keep telling themselves they can manage—when they can't.

WHAT SHOULD COUPLES DO?

Assuming that the ill spouse is mentally competent, couples need to discuss certain things as early in the illness as possible:

How they feel about each other and their changing relationship. It's vital for them to express the grief they're feeling at their losses. If a spouse is not willing or able to hear this, then it's important to find another confidant and let it out. Unexpressed grief will make you mentally, emotionally, and spiritually ill.

The caregiver's need for respite in order to keep going. This means that both the caregiver and the care receiver must be willing to accept respite care, and to spend money on hiring help, if necessary.

Margaret's husband, who had suffered a stroke, wanted to go with her everywhere as he began to recover. "Look," she said, "even employees get two days a week off." She insisted on taking time off without him to do what refreshed and rested her.

But first you have to state the need. Respite is not going to happen unless you plan for it, and perhaps not unless you insist on it.

What are the resources to provide respite? Family? Friends? Community? Are you too proud to ask? Ask anyway. Is there money to hire help? How can you plan so that the money is available? (This is part of financial planning for long-term care—see chapter 20.)

The need for the caregiving spouse to begin to plan for a life alone.

Saying your goodbyes.

Other caregiving tips can be found in my book *Caring for Your Aging Parents: When Love Is Not Enough.*

REBUILDING YOUR LIFE

Bob Foster, widowed less than a year after he retired, found that he had to "rearrange everything" in his life.

"You have to do a lot of introspection or self-analyzing," he said. "I'd always been too busy to stop and think. While I was taking care of my wife, I had plenty of time to think. After she passed away, I became a totally different person. You have to in order to survive."

Widows and widowers may sometimes need to ignore unsolicited advice from well-meaning family and friends. Ruth Nevin tells the widowed, "Evaluate what's being said. You don't have to do it just because they tell you to. How do *you* feel about it? Follow your own feelings."

Ruth continues, "You have a life of your own and so do your children. Children, particularly sons, seem to want to try to take the place of their father. When my first husband died, my oldest son wanted to sit at his place at the dinner table. I said, 'Son, I love you for wanting to help, but you can never be Dad.' And I wouldn't let him sit there. We rearranged the table settings so we wouldn't have to stare at that empty space."

Ruth was wise. Sometimes a widow will transfer her dependence on her late husband to a child, usually a son. This is not healthy for either generation.

Adult children sometimes assume that a widowed parent needs their shelter and protection. The widowed parent may surprise them by remarrying, enlisting in the Peace Corps, or taking up skydiving.

Sometimes adult children disapprove of the changes in a parent. They think that their motivation is the parent's well-being, but they're really resisting change because *they* find it threatening. Young people like their parents to be staid and predictable while *they* have the freedom to experiment. The thought of a parent dating really bothers them.

Adult children may disapprove of remarriage because they feel it's disrespectful to the memory of their dead parent or because they fear the loss of an inheritance. But it's *your* life, not theirs.

GETTING BACK INTO LIFE

Few older singles are eager to get back into the dating game after their grieving is over, but they do want companionship. "Form friendships with members of the opposite sex," Ruth Nevin advises. "There's nothing wrong with that."

Members of our generation may have trouble believing that nonsexual friendships with the opposite sex are possible. But such friendships can be part of the new freedom that widowhood brings. A common interest brings you together. You may see one friend as a dancing partner and another as a bridge partner. And the object need not be matrimony, or even what one of my friends in his seventies calls "fooling around."

What about singles groups? They may not be the ideal place for a woman to find a mate due to the imbalance of the sexes (women over sixty outnumber men over sixty—five to one!), but they do provide a place to find companionship with a group.

SINGLES GROUPS FOR ALL AGES

The Singles Ministry of Lafayette-Orinda Presbyterian Church, one of the country's largest church-sponsored singles organizations, has thousands of participants in the San Francisco Bay area. It offers a Sunday evening lecture series, support groups, and divorce/recovery workshops. But most people join for the social activities, which are divided into three different age groups. There is a calendar of activities to choose from every night of the week—trips and special tours, shared meals, sports (such as sailing, tennis, and skiing), and special interest groups in art, music, theater, and books.

Widows sometimes feel out of place in singles groups that are dominated by divorced people. If so, it's possible to find social groups just for the widowed in many locales.

AN OPPORTUNITY FOR GROWTH

Often, through this process of reentering life, widowed people discover or rediscover interests and aspects of their personalities that they were never able to express in their marriages. That was the case with the widower I know who looked around the home he had shared with his wife and said to himself in wonder, "This is *my* house now." The widowed person no longer has to consult anybody else's wishes.

For most of the widowed, this is not a freedom they had ever wished for. But once it is forced on them, they can often think of plenty of things they like to do that their spouse didn't. Now they can indulge their own tastes.

For widows, being forced to make decisions and to be "in charge" in the absence of their husbands can lead to tremendous personal growth.

Betty Coe used her WPS training in peer counseling to start Christian Widowed Fellowship. Often in the first few years she found herself in over her head. She longed to be able to consult her late husband, who'd had all the counseling skills she needed. *Oh, if only he were here, I'd know what to do,* she thought.

Then she remembered. "You ninny," she told herself. "If he were here, you wouldn't be doing this!" She was growing in the way that most widows grow: not only in spite of the loss but because of it.

SHOULD YOU MOVE?

The widowed often have to struggle with whether or not to live on alone in the home they'd shared with a spouse. Living alone is not for everyone, and sometimes a change proves very beneficial.

At first Anne didn't think she'd like a retirement apartment community where "you see nothing but old people." But after she was widowed, she decided to try it. To her surprise, she found that the planned activities brought her into contact with people who had similar interests. Although her apartment was small, she was able to invite friends and family from outside the retirement community to dine with her in the communal dining hall, and even to arrange special parties for her guests.

She'd thought everything would be done by couples and that she'd be left out. But so many of the residents had been widowed that the number of single women was almost as large as the number of couples. If she wanted to get out into the community as a volunteer, the retirement community had a coordinator who would help her find volunteer work. Transportation was available, paid for by the fee for services that went with her apartment.

Is it never a good idea to live with adult children? In at least two cases that I know of, it's worked out very well. See chapter

9 for the things you and the children need to think about before you make this decision. One suggestion: Try an extended visit on a trial basis before you make the move.

AGE, SEX, AND INCOME

■ Older women outnumber older men, and the gap widens with age. There are eighty-five men per 100 women at ages sixty-five to sixty-nine, but under forty per 100 at age eighty-five-plus. And older women are much more likely than older men to spend their last years in poverty.

■ Twice as many older women live below the poverty line as older men.

■ Jobs held mostly by women are less likely to offer pension plans than jobs held by men.

■ Only 23.8 percent of older women receive pension benefits other than Social Security, compared with 46 percent of older men.

■ Women who have been full-time homemakers often lose their rights to a husband's pension when they are divorced or widowed.

■ Homemakers receive no Social Security credit for their years at home. Women who take time out of the work force to raise children or care for elderly parents lose years that count toward Social Security and pensions. So they can look forward to lower retirement incomes.

■ The number of "displaced homemakers" increased 12 percent in the 1980s, up from 13.9 million in 1980 to 15.6 million in 1989. These divorced or widowed women are too young to receive Social Security payments, but too old to find adequate jobs.[1]

SPECIAL PROBLEMS OF WIDOWS

Students of human behavior as well as those who work with the widowed agree: Widowers seem to have more difficulty in adjusting than widows. Researchers believe that women's better ability to cope with being single is related to their greater ability to form intimate relationships with others besides their mates.[2] Also, since there are many more widows than widowers, it's much easier for women to have friends of the same sex to confide in.

But widows on the average have more financial problems than widowers. The likelihood for women to become poor rises with age, especially for those who depend solely on Social Security or their husband's pension for retirement income. A husband's pension ends or is cut in half when he dies. The wife's assets can be wiped out by her husband's final illness or nursing home costs.

"Displaced homemakers" are women who are widowed or divorced before they are old enough to qualify for Social Security and who have no job skills. Nobody ever thinks it will happen to them. One evening, Carol, who serves meals at a shelter for the homeless, started a conversation with a woman who was around her own age. To her shock, she found out that this intelligent fifty-five-year-old woman was destitute because her husband of thirty years had recently divorced her. She had no skills, was not able to get a job except part-time work at minimum wage, and had used up all her savings. "A year ago, I was just like you," the woman told Carol sadly.

SPECIAL PROBLEMS OF WIDOWERS

Men in our society find losses difficult to cope with, and men suffering from depression also find it difficult to ask for help. All their lives, they've been told, "Be a man. Be strong." This makes becoming widowed extremely difficult for them.

Ironically, the "stronger" men act, the weaker they actually become. A study of over 7,000 adults by Maradee Davis, an epidemiologist at the University of California San Francisco revealed that men who lived alone or with someone other than a spouse were twice as likely to die within ten years as men of the same age who lived with a spouse.

Elderly men depend almost exclusively on their wives for proper diet, social life, and emotional support. Often widowers remarry quickly so they can be taken care of. (And some later regret these hasty marriages, which often end in divorce.)

SUICIDE IN ELDERLY MEN

In a different study, many men surveyed listed their wives as their only confidant. A confidant is considered essential to mental health in aging people. Most women tended to have one in addition to their husbands. For a man who has no one else to confide in, the loss of his wife is devastating.

According to an AARP study published in 1989, white males over sixty-five have the highest rate of suicide in the United States, 43.2 per 100,000, or nearly four times the national average. During the decade of the eighties, the suicide rate for elderly men increased 25 percent. The actual rate may be somewhat higher, according to Marv Miller, the author of *Suicide After Sixty*, since elderly suicides are usually under-reported.

Women who live alone or with someone other than a spouse are also more likely to die within ten years compared to others the same age living with a spouse. But suicide does not increase rapidly with age in women as it does in men. Researchers linked women's increased risk of death to their low income, which denied them adequate food, medicine, or health care.

SINGLE OLDER ADULTS

- Widows aged sixty-five and older in the United States: 7.5 million
- Widowers aged sixty-five and older in the U.S.: 1.2 million
- Widows aged fifty-five to sixty-four: an additional 2 million
- Widowers aged fifty-five to sixty-four: an additional 355,000
- Remarriage rates for widows over sixty-five: 2 per 1000
- Remarriage rates for widowers over sixty-five: 20 per 1000
- Remarriage rates for divorced women over sixty-five: 9 per 1000
- Remarriage rates for divorced men over sixty-five: 31 per 1000[3]

CAN YOU PREPARE FOR WIDOWHOOD?

Can a person prepare for losing his or her spouse? I think the answer to that question is yes and no. It's certainly necessary and prudent to prepare financially for widowhood. But I'm not sure that you can ever prepare emotionally for becoming widowed (just writing this chapter was difficult for me). But there are some practical steps that everyone can take to prepare. One is cross-training each other (see chapter 10).

Widowhood is a little easier if both husband and wife have developed separate interests and friends. If couples have only "couple friends" whom they see only together, never as individuals, these types of friendships tend to disappear with the marriage. Widowhood may then leave the remaining spouse bereft of friends.

Often both sexes are trapped in stultifying, stereotyped sex roles. Men have been taught that needing help is unmanly, and that men are supposed to be self-sufficient. Women have been taught that asking for anything for yourself is unwomanly, that you're supposed to satisfy others' needs and never your own. One sex needs to become more emotionally open and the other, more assertive.

At widowhood, it's change or perish. We all need to acquire

the attitude of the widow who said, "I've never been one to sit down on a stool in an empty field and wait for a cow to back up to me. You have to go after what you need."

QUESTIONS FOR DISCUSSION

1. Are you financially prepared for widowhood?
2. If you should become widowed, who would you turn to? Is there someone you can talk to about your feelings?
3. How would you feel if your spouse were forced to place you in a nursing home? Are you financially prepared for this?
4. The Bible teaches compassion and care for the widow and the orphan. What is your church doing for its widowed members?
5. How could you or your church serve the special needs of both widowed men and widowed women?

CHAPTER TWELVE

THE ENDURING POWER OF FRIENDSHIPS

Making new friends and maintaining friendships as we age is more important to our morale than even family relationships.
Rebecca G. Adams and Rosemary Blieszner, *Older Adult Friendships*

Retirement, as a turning point in life, presents us with more free time to make new friends. At the same time, we may lose (or at the very least, loosen our ties with) friends from work.

After thirty-seven years as a social worker with Los Angeles County, Hilda felt it was time to retire. Her elderly, widowed mother was finding it more difficult to live alone in her own home. So Hilda, who had been widowed herself for many years, moved in with her mother (in another city) to take care of her. Except for her brother, she had no other family.

It was hard for Hilda to leave her coworkers behind. As is so often the case with single people, she considered the people she worked with to be like her family. In addition, she had to say goodbye to good neighbors she'd known for thirty-eight years. She had watched their children grow up. Hilda was also a very active member of her church.

These ties were her support system. We all have them. Unfortunately we tend to take them for granted until they're no longer there (or until we suddenly become single after a spouse dies and we really need them).

The adjustment was not easy. Caregiving responsibilities made it difficult for Hilda to get out and meet new people or become active in the life of her mother's congregation. How *did* she cope?

Her mother's neighbors were supportive and friendly, which helped. Also, Hilda reached out to a support group for widows and another for caregivers, and through these groups she made new friends. She attended a class cosponsored by AARP on financial management for women. She renewed the close relationship that she'd had with her brother when they were children. Her sister-in-law and nieces also became her friends. By the time her mother died and her caregiving responsibilities had ended, Hilda had built a new support network of friends and acquaintances to replace the one she'd lost. She now lives alone, but she is not lonely.

ALONE, BUT NOT LONELY

More people than ever are living alone. Statistically, at least, it doesn't seem to be a very healthy lifestyle for the elderly. But alone doesn't necessarily mean lonely. Loneliness is more of a *feeling* about being alone. It has more to do with our health and our spiritual condition than with objective fact.

In a study of aging persons in three countries (the United States, Great Britain, and Denmark), people who said that their health was poor were much more likely to report that they often felt lonely *regardless of whether or not they were living alone.*[1] Perhaps this means that because of illness, they are no longer able to get out and be with their friends.

FRIENDSHIP AND MENTAL HEALTH

The ability to make and keep friends helps us cope with the many changes that come with age. There are no substitutes for the special relationships we have with our friends.

What friends do for us raises our self-esteem more than what family members do for us because it's not "expected," explain sociologists Susan Crohan and Toni Antonucci. From friends we get emotional support, love, admiration, validation of our feelings, and affirmation of who we are, as well as information and practical aid. Being able to give to friends in return also raises our self-esteem.

Each friend contributes something different. We learn from friends all our lives. Women, especially, credit their friends with helping their personal growth. Evelyn, for example, learned from her friend Nancy, who was dying of cancer, how to enjoy each moment. One beautiful spring day long after Nancy had died, Evelyn took time out to savor the flowers and the balmy air, and said, "Isn't this wonderful? I'm loving it. Nancy, this is for you!"

And so, the benefits of a friendship can live on after a friend is gone. Even if an elderly person has few friends still living, the memories of past friendships can continue to nourish his spirit.

WHAT'S THE SECRET?

Why do some aging people seem to have friends all their lives while others become isolated and lonely? Often in extreme old age there are circumstances over which one has no control. But there are other factors as well.

Sarah H. Matthews interviewed sixty-three men and women over sixty on the topic of friendship. From her data, she identified three "friendship styles" that influence how people make and keep friends.[2] She named these "styles":

The independent. These people consider themselves self-sufficient. They have many acquaintances, but are reluctant to name anybody as a close friend. Circumstances dictate who their associates will be. When circumstances change, so do their "friends." Their relationships lack commitment. They purposely keep them superficial, either because they do not trust people or because they do not trust themselves.

The discerning. These people identify a small number of people to whom they feel really close. They tend to have one or two "ideal friendships," often from early in their lives, which no other relationship could measure up to. One person surveyed gave the impression that when he had reached adulthood, he'd put away childish things, friendship being one of them.

The acquisitive. These are people who move throughout their lives collecting a variety of friendships, committing themselves to friendships once they are made. Unlike the discerning, they are open to acquiring new friends. They see each new turning point in life (such as retirement) as an opportunity to acquire new friends, without having to give up the old ones. When distances separate them from old friends, they maintain affectionate ties and reactivate the friendships if circumstances permit. These people draw their friends from a variety of sources.

FRIENDSHIPS AS INVESTMENTS

Matthews also characterizes the three groups by the time periods they emphasize. "Independents" focus on the present, "discerners" on the past, and "acquisitives" have both past and present friends but also look to the future.

You can think of friends as "investments," a kind of bank account. As you age, the account goes down. Even if you stay put, friends move away. Death and disabilities—especially mental ones that affect the ability to communicate—take away other friends. Friendships built around an activity (such as golf) may end when you are no longer physically able to participate. Lack of transportation or mobility may also make visiting your friends difficult or impossible.

Also, there are no guarantees that friends will be there for you when you need them. Friends can also be lost when a relationship dies of neglect or abuse. The only way to protect yourself is to keep adding to the account all the time. As you age, the "pool" from which you can draw friends your own age declines, but the wise older person gets around a major part of this dilemma by having younger friends.

MAKING YOUNGER FRIENDS

I think of people who have developed friendships with younger people. Martha has kept up a friendship with a young man who boarded with her family when he was in college. Anna still goes to art galleries with the little boy she taught in first grade, who grew up to become an artist. Ruth has many friends among the younger women she's taught in Bible Study Fellowship. Many older people make friends of their adult children (more about that in the next chapter).

The people I see making younger friends usually start in middle age by *mentoring* younger people. They become a younger person's wise counselor, teacher, and guide. Often these are work-connected relationships (although the friendships may continue outside of the work setting). After retirement you may really need to get creative to find a way of making younger friends.

CREATIVE NURTURING TIME

Elizabeth (Liz) Marcellin and Nancy Payton, two women whose children are grown, remembered how frazzled they felt as young mothers. They wanted to do something for younger women that would be fun. So they came up with an idea that they call "Creative Nurturing Time." One evening a month, they open Liz's home to any women who want to come. Each month, fifteen to twenty women show up.

Liz puts out a few simple craft materials and refreshments, and the younger women are free to do whatever they wish. One young mother got her heart's desire: to soak in the bathtub and do her hair without having children clamoring outside her door. Others relax in the spa, play the piano, work on a craft project, or just sit and talk. Often, there's an opportunity for Liz or Nancy to help one of the younger women with a word of advice or encouragement. By following the words of Titus 2:3-5 ("The older women . . . can train the younger women . . ."), they've enriched both generations.

NEGATIVE ATTITUDES THAT HURT US

Yet some older people feel that "only somebody my age is capable of understanding me." An elderly man once said to a very young social worker, "Young lady, I have corns that are older than you are!" It was a putdown delivered as a joke, but a putdown all the same.

Out of fear of being rejected by the young, some older people practice a kind of reverse ageism. At a writer's conference, I overheard a writer a little older than myself lambaste the editor of a retirement magazine for having a woman in her forties on his staff. "How could anyone that young relate to my needs?" she demanded to know.

I was embarrassed. How could anybody who had lived so long be so shortsighted? But this behavior is typical of any group that feels threatened or rejected by the culture at large: We retreat into our little ghetto and talk only to ourselves.

If you want to have friends when you age, don't make this mistake!

DIFFERENT FRIENDS FOR DIFFERENT NEEDS

Not surprisingly, Matthews' "acquisitives" have the best friendship style for getting the support they need in old age. Their ability to focus on all three time periods (past, present, and future) means that they have the three types of friends that sociologist

Eugene Litvak says older people need.

Everybody needs *long-term friends* because we all need people who "knew us when" in order to confirm our identity. We're not just the people you see in the present. We're also the little girl on roller skates, the high school football player, the Girl Scout leader thirty years ago, the first organizer of a church's Sunday school, and much, much more.

Even though we seldom see these old friends, we tend to feel extremely close to them. It amazed me, when I moved to California, that I was able to renew a friendship with Clare, a college friend I hadn't seen in thirty years. We were able to pick right up where we left off without missing a beat. On a visit to New York, I spent time with another childhood friend whom I hadn't seen in years. Her mother, then in her eighties, and I spent most of a day going through old photo albums and reminiscing. It was good for both of us.

Some long-term friends might be family members—siblings, cousins, or in-laws whom we can potentially become closer to. Frequently, widowed brothers and sisters become very good friends in old age, renewing their youthful relationship with the person who best "knew them when" because they grew up in the same household.

Intermediate friends are those we make over a lifetime as our roles change—at various jobs we hold, the friends we make when our children are in school (often the parents of *their* friends), or when we move to a new neighborhood or a new town. They may be our friends for a long time, but not all of them are retained over a lifetime.

Short-term friends are the new ones that we make. Research reveals that, health permitting, older people can continue to make new friends all their lives. This is encouraging. But the elderly need opportunities for friendship. The setting one is in does make a difference. One advantage of retirement communities is that they provide opportunities for new friendships among the residents who would otherwise be isolated.

Churches also have a role to play. I know it's fashionable in some circles to denigrate church activities for seniors as "putting them in a playpen." But older people who begin meeting socially can often evolve into a support network. They become friends who help each other when illnesses and losses come.

THE ROLE PLAYED BY PETS

Jame Quackenbush, a social worker, comments, "Most owners aren't aware their pets offer them an unusual type of friendship that's not available elsewhere. . . . Your pet can be whatever you want him to be, and generally will never fail to meet your expectations. . . . A pet stays with you in good times and bad, always listens to you, and usually acts as if he understands and sympathizes with what you're saying. . . . As a result your pet contributes to your sense of social stability. He's predictable, dependable, giving you a critical sense of emotional balance on an everyday basis."[3]

Pets have a calming effect on our emotions—researchers have found that stroking an animal actually lowers a person's blood pressure. Pets are companions, "security blankets," even surrogate children.

Just as people need to be nurtured, they have powerful needs to nurture. As my mother-in-law said about her cat, "I must have something to take care of."

A pet can be a link with a dead loved one, and be the center of a world of memories—a powerful source of comfort to a grieving widow or widower, and wonderful company for people living alone.

Unfortunately, many retirement communities do not allow pets. To have to give up a pet, either because you must move or because the pet dies, can be the cause of intense grief that many people don't seem to understand.

MEN'S SPECIAL PROBLEMS WITH FRIENDSHIP

Friendships with others of the same sex seem to be easier for women than for men. Women grow up placing more value on personal relationships and sharing their feelings with each other. But men tend to have "workmates" or "golfing buddies," and no close personal friends but their wives. Unless men develop new interests after retirement, they will have no new friends. Since there are fewer and fewer surviving men in each older age group, retired men tend to become more solitary and socially isolated than retired women.

And so, as they age, older men have fewer friends than older women to act as a buffer against the sorrows of life. In the Matthews sample, more men than women were either "independent" or "discerning" in their friendship styles. Many married men depend on their wives to make "couple friends" for both of them. But even if couples do not drop their widowed friends (which is a very common occurrence), most widowed people are not comfortable participating in activities dominated by married couples. If the wife dies first, the husband reverts to being a loner.

WHERE CAN MEN "HANG OUT"?

Older men, perhaps more than older women, seem to need some place to "hang out" together. When I was a college student, Washington Square Park in New York City was filled during the warmer months with retirees playing checkers or chess.

The old-fashioned barbershop used to be a traditional masculine hangout where men of all ages gathered, but barbershops have largely been replaced by unisex haircutters. In some small towns and suburban areas, a local coffee shop often becomes a hangout where retirees (mostly male) settle world affairs at their morning bull sessions. But many of these are closing down, too.

Many communities have Senior Centers that attempt to provide a gathering place, but they're usually under-utilized by the over-sixty-five bunch. Some seniors are turned off by the programs. Others think they're only for low-income seniors. Sometimes, the membership is so predominantly female that men just won't go to them.

What is the answer?

One of our friends belongs to the "Sons of Retirement," a club that meets once a month for lunch and speakers. According to its members, it "has absolutely no redeeming social value." But that's okay with the people who attend.

One local church sponsors twice-monthly breakfast meetings for male retirees. This group, too, is strictly social. "It replaces the water cooler at the office," says one member. A similar weekly breakfast club, but for widowers only, meets on Saturday mornings at a Denver restaurant.

The greatest detriment to investing in friendships as we age seems to be inertia: the tendency that begins in middle age to keep us in our accustomed ruts. Both men *and* women get this way, and they need some kind of stimulus to get them moving again. In the final analysis, the way to have the friends you need as you age is no different for men than it is for women—that is, to pay attention to friendships in the early retirement years and to adopt some of the following strategies that seem to work:

1. *Get involved in activities that bring you into contact with new people.*
2. *Keep in contact with friends you already have, by mail and phone if you can't see them frequently.*
3. *Reactivate old friendships and renew neglected family contacts.*
4. *Make friends with family members, especially adult children and siblings.*
5. *Try to reach out to people both older and younger than yourself, building relationships up and down the generational ladder.*

GOD, OUR CLOSEST FRIEND

One practical step we can take, in addition to working on friendships after retirement, is to learn how to spend time alone. Instead of being lonely, we could learn to *enjoy* solitude and to use it as an opportunity for spiritual growth.

No matter how many friends we have, the sobering truth is that as we age, fewer of our friends will survive with us. Our own illness or frailty may mean that we will have to spend a great deal of time alone. We will be fortunate, then, if we have learned to view solitude not as a punishment but as an opportunity to get closer to God, who is our friend of friends.

Jesus said, "I no longer call you servants. . . . Instead, I have called you friends" (John 15:15). David cried out that all his other friends had abandoned him—one whom he especially trusted had betrayed him—but God was still with him (Psalm 41:9-12)!

Often the depth of a relationship with God can be plumbed only when human relationships fade away. It is then that prayer—talking to and listening to God—takes on a new purpose and meaning. Loneliness is often a choice. Those who have accepted God's invitation to friendship have really *chosen* not to be lonely in old age.

QUESTIONS FOR DISCUSSION

1. What is your "friendship style"?
2. Make a list of your long-term, intermediate, and short-term friends. Are there any old relationships that you could reactivate?
3. Do you need more new friends? How will you find them?
4. Are there any lonely people older than yourself whom you could befriend?
5. What could you do to reach out to and encourage a younger person or persons who could become your friends?

CHAPTER THIRTEEN

ONCE A PARENT, ALWAYS A PARENT

Children begin loving their parents;
after a time they judge them;
rarely, if ever, do they forgive them.
Oscar Wilde

You may think you can retire from being a parent. But no matter what your adult children are like—whether they are a source of pleasure or of pain, whether relations with them are cordial, strained, or even broken—*families are forever*. Despite what Oscar Wilde said, members of a family *can* forgive each other. In fact, the longer lifespan of parents nowadays gives families more opportunities than ever to mend their relationships.

The feeling that you're still a parent is normal and even desirable. Lynn White of the University of Nebraska and John Edwards of Virginia Polytechnic Institute found that "continuation of the parental role appears to be important to parental well-being. . . . Twenty to twenty-five years of active parenthood leaves a mark on relationships and individual personalities that cannot be eliminated simply because the children are gone."[1]

Once a parent, always a parent. But hopefully, not the same kind of parent. Our adult children are no longer (we hope) dependent children, but fellow adults and friends.

DELAYED INDEPENDENCE

Achieving a more equal relationship with our adult children is sometimes delayed because, to restate the obvious, our children are very different from the way we were at their age. Evidence from research suggests that today's young adults are taking longer than we did to reach independence from parents. Seldom is this accomplished before they're in their thirties.

Young people today are leaving home later, getting married later, and having their first child later than our generation did. If we expect them to follow *our* timetable, we're bound to be disappointed.

In fact, they may still need to establish their independence from us at the very time that we begin to think about our own aging and want more attention from them. There is some danger that our need for them could keep them dependent longer, delaying their adult development.

The 1990 census revealed that 32 percent of single men and 20 percent of single women ages twenty-five to thirty-four lived with their parents. This compares to 9.4 percent of men and 6.6 percent of all women in this age group in 1970. The major cause of this dramatic change is economic. Young people under twenty-five experienced a 10 percent drop in income during the 1980s, and three out of four young men ages eighteen to twenty-four are still living at home.

The younger group may still be in school, but some of the older young people are the so-called "boomerang kids," those who left home and returned for reasons such as a divorce or a job loss.

This is quite different from our generation's experiences. We came of age and raised our families during a time of rapid economic expansion. We may have had help from the G.I. bill in going to college or buying our first home; most of our children don't. We expected to have job security; today, layoffs are routine. Young people today are more like their Depression-era grandparents than like our generation. Once again, as in those difficult days several decades ago, families may have to learn to pull together in order to survive.

HOW MUCH FINANCIAL HELP?

The challenge is, how much financial help, if any, should you give adult children? And how will you know if your help is actually damaging to them?

Some researchers have speculated that more men than women are living at home because they're getting a free ride from mom.

They get home cooking, laundry, and maid service in much nicer surroundings than they could afford independently. Some really can't support themselves, but others are just taking advantage of living at home so that they can spend their salaries on expensive cars, electronic toys, and vacations. Are you willing to support this lifestyle on a retirement income? Should you? Are you in fact doing the child a disservice by protecting him from the harsh realities of paying his own bills?

Between the child who could make it on his own but won't and the child who was laid off and whose family could end up homeless unless you help, there are vast gray areas. It's important that parents set limits—a time limit if a move back home is temporary, or a dollar limit of what they can afford to do.

OTHER FORMS OF HELP

There are other forms of help besides financial ones. Often gifts of time, rather than money, are win-win deals for both generations, and don't encourage over-dependence. Babysitting, an enormous help to young parents, benefits the older generation by bringing them closer to grandchildren. Home repair is another area of service to young families. Many retired dads bring their tools along on visits and help their adult children with needed repairs they can't afford to pay for.

You can be a volunteer with your own children. Eleanor and Frank are spending a lot of time in their retirement years helping their youngest son in his retail store. And so he gets valuable, trustworthy employees he could never afford to hire, and they get a break from caring for Frank's aged mother in their home.

Instead of "coming to the rescue" financially, you might be able to tell your adult children where they could get funds elsewhere. Instead of giving their son and daughter-in-law the down payment for a house, the MacDonalds showed them how they could get a lease-option on a house through a realtor they knew.

WHAT CAN YOU AFFORD?

Other parents, older and foreseeing less need for the money in the future, offered the down payment for a house to their son and daughter-in-law without even being asked. "You've never asked for anything," Hal said, "but I want you to have this house now while you have a growing family and need it, instead of leaving it to you in my will."

Neither parents were either right or wrong in their approach. They did what they thought was right and what felt comfortable to them.

Nevertheless, money either given or withheld can cause a lot of family bitterness in the future. If you decide to help financially, make sure you clarify whether the money is a gift or a loan. The experts say that "loans" between family members are seldom repaid, so if you really need the money, you'd better get a legally enforceable note. And if it is a loan, can you afford not to get it back or to give up the income that this money is bringing in? If you can't, are you willing to sue your own child to get the money back?

Also be aware that if you give a child a gift of more than $10,000 in any one year, say accountants, you will be subject to a federal gift tax.

WHAT ABOUT INHERITANCES?

Europe in the Middle Ages and well into the nineteenth century had an unwritten family contract: Care for the frail elderly parent in return for an inheritance, whether it is the family farm, a business, or cash. Old people who had no families were allowed to die of neglect or were taken care of (although not very well) by the local municipality or county. That pattern carried over into the United States, and vestiges of these expectations are still with us today.

Most older people, however, do not want to be taken care of by their children. Anna and Charlie had made arrangements to enter a retirement home that provides full services because they saw the day coming when they would not be able to manage on their own. But such a move would take all their money. When they told their oldest son, he said, "Oh, don't do that. We'll take care of you!" But Anna, who had taken care of both of *her* parents at considerable cost to her peace of mind and health, said, "You don't realize what you're saying!" She knew that they were likely to pay much too high a price for this inheritance.

It's important to communicate your financial needs in retirement to your children. We've told our three grown children that our goal is to avoid becoming a financial burden to *them* in our old age. We will most likely use all our financial resources for that purpose, and it's not likely they'll inherit very much.

Some older people dangle a promised inheritance in front of their children, but the reality today is that only the very wealthy can be sure there will be any inheritance left, if they have to enter a nursing home. Financial promises to your children that you may not be able to keep are better not made.

WE NEED TO CHANGE

Keeping adult children financially dependent on us is one way of hanging on to control, instead of working toward a more equal relationship. But there are other ways in which we try to control our children, such as criticizing them (making them feel inadequate) or playing on their sympathy (making them feel guilty). In the long run, this kind of manipulation always backfires.

Some families are still "stuck" in old patterns of parental favoritism or sibling rivalry for their parents' attention. Adult children with unresolved sibling rivalries may try to earn brownie points with you by running each other down. Some parents actually encourage this behavior because they feel, consciously or unconsciously, that if the children vie for their favor, they'll get more attention.

This is what my mother-in-law used to call "storing up trouble for yourself in the future." Just wait until they start fighting about whether or not to put you in a nursing home! Believe me, it's in your own best interests to encourage them to be friends with each other.

GETTING CAUGHT IN THE MIDDLE

The myth of "one big happy family" dies hard, which probably explains why so many family members go to large holiday gatherings with high expectations and go away disappointed, hurt, and upset year after year. But look at a family realistically: With so many people involved, it would be surprising if there *weren't* differences. It's not your job to make all these people love each other or even get along.

Beware of the temptation to let them communicate with each other through you, a pattern I see in many families. A good rule of communication is, "Talk *to* each other, not *about* each other." Encourage your adult children to talk to each other, not you, about their own differences.

WHEN YOUR CHILDREN DIVORCE

Divorce can tear families apart. If you love your child's spouse, must you give him or her up if they divorce? Do you have to take sides? Ethel's son was extremely angry with his mother for keeping up a relationship with his ex-wife. "But I didn't divorce her, he did," she said. "Besides, she's the mother of my grandchildren, and I certainly don't want to lose *them*. He'll get over it."

Step-families also complicate matters. "My children are into the arts, and his children are into sports," says Marsha, who has been married to her second husband, Ben, for only five years. "It's not that they dislike each other, but they have nothing in common."

One option would be to provide activities at family gatherings that get everyone involved doing things together instead of sitting around trying to make conversation. Games, sports, and music are all possibilities. In one family, the children put on little plays for everybody. There's a lot of joking and laughter. Silly party games—the sillier the better—get people laughing and lighten everybody's mood.

If none of this works, it might be better to see warring family members separately from each other. If they want to get along better, let them take the responsibility for reconciliation.

TREAT THEM LIKE FRIENDS

Relationships with adult children and their spouses really boil down to this: How would you treat a friend you loved? Would you criticize and discourage him, or would you give him emotional support and encouragement? The answer is obvious. But does this mean you can never speak frankly to an adult child?

Here's a principle I like, which applies as well to adult children and their spouses as it does to your friends: "If it's very painful for you to criticize your friends—you're safe in doing it. But if you take the slightest pleasure in it—that's the time to hold your tongue."[2] When in doubt, the safest thing to do is *not* to work on changing your children, but rather on changing yourself.

REMEMBER WHAT IT WAS LIKE FOR YOU

It amazes me how quickly older people develop amnesia about the pressures of young adult life. Don't you remember how harried you were when you were with little children twenty-four hours a day? Didn't you worry about being able to pay your bills? Didn't you hate it when your parents told you what to do—as if you were an idiot? Then how come we're doing the same things to our own children that our parents did to us?

When we're together, both parents and adult children tend to fall back into their old roles. Habit takes over. Often adult children reawaken our old parenting routines by acting like ten-year-olds whenever we're around. Our views of each other tend to get frozen. For example, your child may still be carrying around an image of the tyrant who wouldn't get him a pony for his tenth birthday. You may be carrying around an image of an irresponsible teenager who wouldn't clean his room. These phantoms from the past will go away only when we learn who this person is *now*, not who he or she used to be many years ago.

STEP BACK, NOT OUT

Acceptance is the key to letting go of an obsolete past relationship and forging a new one more in keeping with the present needs of both generations. You don't have to step completely out of their lives and leave your adult children feeling abandoned, but you may have to learn to back off a little.

I thought I had let go when my children were in college, but I really hadn't. I still had the unconscious feeling that my young adult children were my "unfinished projects," and that it was my duty to polish away any flaws I perceived. What madness! Who put me in charge of requiring perfection of anybody else? Or as Jesus put it so eloquently, "First take the plank out of your own eye, and then you will see clearly to remove the speck from your brother's eye" (Matthew 7:5).

At some point, I had to realize that no matter what *I* wanted for them, my adult children had to learn from their mistakes—just as I did. I believe that God allows us to make mistakes so that we *can* learn. So who was I to interfere with His work in my children's lives? They are exactly who they have chosen to be on their way to becoming whoever they will be. That realization brought me peace.

Adult children *feel* your unspoken demands. Letting go of these demands takes some of the pressure off them and makes a better relationship at least a possibility (although not a certainty).

WHAT ABOUT IN-LAWS?

The same acceptance that you practice with your children is also the key to a better relationship with their spouses. Can you remember what it felt like when you were first married? Weren't you scared? Didn't you wonder, *Will this new family like me? Will we get along?* These memories should inspire compassion. Remember, your new daughter-in-law and son-in-law are probably more afraid of you than you are of them! It's a rare young person who isn't grateful for kindness and warmth.

I was fortunate to have wonderful in-laws as role models. My husband's parents were unfailingly loving and never interfered. Because of their non-interference, when they did speak up, I listened. I knew, "This must be important or they wouldn't say anything." By letting little things go, they had earned the right to be heard on important matters. They had won my respect as well as my love.

Acceptance does not mean you approve of everything your children and their spouses do. You may even have to say, "Look, I can't agree with this, but you're an adult and you don't need my approval. Let's agree to disagree, but continue to love each other."

However, because the young are still uncertain and insecure (especially in sensitive areas such as money management or child-rearing), they may still unconsciously be seeking your approval and feel very threatened if you disagree with them.

If you can convey a feeling of warmth and acceptance to both children and in-laws, mistakes are much more easily forgiven. And yes, it is possible to love these in-laws, even when you start off not liking them very much.

I like my friend Betty's attitude: "She's not the wife *I* would have chosen for him, but I don't have to live with her. She makes my son happy, and that's what's important. I'd accept her even if she had two heads!"

ARE YOU ANGRY AT YOUR CHILDREN?

Are you angry at your children for the way they've messed up their lives? This is understandable, considering how many of the baby boom generation have left behind a trail of drug addiction, unstable job histories, divorce, and deserted children. Some of these former prodigals have returned and have become, much to their parents' amazement, productive workers and exemplary parents. I can think of several in our church. Frankly, it's a miracle that they're still alive. To their parents' credit, they welcomed these prodigals back with open arms.

Do your children blame you for their problems? This is a common pattern. In some cases, they may be right. Jim was an alcoholic during his daughter Cassie's childhood. The damage his behavior caused is very evident in her troubled marriage and erratic parenting. She wants nothing to do with her dad, who is now in recovery, but he has established a relationship with Cassie's husband, Mark. Jim can help Mark understand why Cassie acts the way she does. "I didn't raise her right," he admits. But even though he freely admits this and has asked his daughter's forgiveness, Jim has no power to change her. It's her responsibility to straighten out her own life.

Counseling may help. Competent counselors will not allow their clients to cop out by blaming their parents. They will try to help them work through their anger and take hold of their own lives. (Many recommend the book *Making Peace with Your Parents* by Bloomfield and Felder. It may be appropriate for you to suggest it to your own angry children.) But your wallowing in guilt can't change the past or do your adult children any good. Getting on with their lives is *their* job, not yours.

WHY WON'T SOME PARENTS LET GO?

Life for some parents remains a battle they are determined to win, even if it means defeating their own children. Their self-esteem depends on feeling superior to their child.

Sam, sixty-eight and retired, was telling his son, Jack, thirty-five, who'd recently started a new job, war stories from his own career, sprinkled with advice on handling the politics of his new job. The dominant phrase that I recall was, "You'd better . . ."

Sam's advice was sound, but that's beside the point. The message that I was hearing between the lines was, "You'll never be the man I am, and you're not as smart as I am, so you'll never be successful unless you do what I say." Jack was well aware of the hidden message his father was sending, and he reacted with anger. The evening ended in a battle royal between father and son.

Perhaps Sam thought he was "helping" his son with his new

job. But he was doing it in a way that no younger person could accept. Like a lot of advice-giving, it was really a putdown. What was wrong?

DEVELOPING "GENERATIVITY"

Sam essentially failed to achieve a crucial task of the middle years. Erik Erikson, who developed the idea that our life journey consists of stages we all go through from birth to death, calls this task of the middle years "generativity," which means entering into "nurturing" or "mentoring" kinds of relationships. The opposite of "generativity" in Erikson's theory is "stagnation," going round and round in the same old rut. Sam, for example, is still stuck in the behavior he learned as a young man, competing with his son instead of encouraging him.

The change from focusing on our own individual achievement and competing to win, which everybody in our society learns at an early age, to a new attitude of *building for a future we will not be part of* is absolutely necessary if we are to age successfully.

The virtue that emerges from "generativity," according to Erikson, is "care," which is not too different from the Christian virtue of charity. The opposite of "care" is "rejectivity," in which we may reject the whole younger population, including but not limited to our own children.[3]

INVESTING IN FAMILY RELATIONSHIPS

The problem with rejecting the younger generation is that there are more of them than there are of us. If you live long enough, friends your own age will die off and you'll be left alone. Then, if not before, you'll begin missing your children if you're estranged from them. Then, if not before, you'll probably want more from your family than the polite but distant relationship you may be settling for now.

Relationships are like money: If you want to have any in the future, you have to start investing now.

Not long ago, a small group I belong to was studying the book of Ecclesiastes. I was leading the session on chapter 11, which begins, "Cast your bread upon the waters . . ." As an opening question, I asked the group, "Aside from money, what was the best investment you ever made?" The answers surprised me.

A young adult said, "Investing the time in building a relationship with my mother." A woman in her seventies said, "Repairing the relationship with my oldest daughter." And the response of a middle-aged man was, "Healing the relationship I had with my daughters when they were growing up." No other investment of their time, they said, had given them greater benefits.

Either generation can take the initiative, but it's interesting that in two out of three of these cases, it was the older (and supposedly wiser) generation that took the first step. Perhaps it's because we're most aware, or should be, that the time we have left to mend relationships is drawing to a close.

"My father finally wised up and called my brother on his birthday," my friend Erika said. "They haven't spoken for eight years. I'm glad he finally did it, but why did it have to take eight years?"

Pride perhaps. Or a lack of courage. Some older people are helped by a family go-between who will approach an estranged family member and say, "Are you open to a call?" Such overtures are seldom refused. However, if you try for a reconciliation and don't succeed, don't give up. There is always hope that this child will later have a change of heart.

COMMUNICATE YOUR WISHES

One thing that I learned from caring for my parents as they aged was the importance of communicating your own wishes about late-life care to adult children before a crisis occurs. Naturally, it's a lot easier to talk to adult children about these sensitive matters if you have a good relationship.

What do parents need to talk to their adult children about? Some important issues are: *What are your plans if you should become unable to care for yourselves? How much money is available for your care? Where are your important documents kept? Who will be your executor? What are your wishes regarding being kept alive on life support? What are your funeral arrangements?*

Unless you give clear directions, decisions will have to be made for you by your next of kin. You may not like these decisions, but you have nobody to blame but yourselves because you could have done something before it was too late and you didn't.

I've seen too many families torn apart by disagreements over "what to do about Mom and Dad"; too many guilt-stricken caregivers whose parents extracted impossible-to-keep promises of "Don't ever put me into a nursing home"; too much stress caused by parents who expected adult children to take over responsibility for them while *they* tried to retain all the control; too much pain that could have been avoided if only the old people hadn't been so secretive about money.

I've often thought, "Maybe I'll get that way, too, when I get old. Maybe I won't be as mentally sharp as I am now." So the time to talk about these things is *now*. Tell your children, "This is what I want you to do. Later on, I may change, become demanding and unreasonable, lose my ability to think or to make decisions. Pay no attention to me then, but do what I want done *now*, while I am in my right mind."

QUESTIONS FOR DISCUSSION

1. Do you feel comfortable talking to your adult children about money? Why, or why not?
2. Have you talked to your adult children about your own future care?
3. Is there any relationship with an adult child that *you* need to work on?
4. Did your relationship with an adult child's spouse get off on the wrong foot? What, if anything, has helped?
5. Is there anything about you that needs to change before a relationship can change?

CHAPTER FOURTEEN

LET YOUR CHILDREN KNOW WHO YOU ARE

Time present and time past
Are both perhaps present in time future,
And time future is contained in time past.
T. S. Eliot, *Four Quartets*

Our children may think they know us because we raised them, yet they don't really know us at all. The parental role is only one part of our lives. We had an existence before the children came along, and God willing, we'll still have one after they leave home.

Besides, each child in a family knows a slightly different parent, as Erma Bombeck once pointed out in a hilarious column she called "The Three Faces of Mom." Her child number one got the "Antiseptic Queen," who boiled pacifiers, toys, and cloth diapers, and took pictures at least every four days for the baby album. Child number two got "Super Sufferer," who had stretch marks on her face from overeating. If the pacifier dropped, she rinsed it with a garden hose. Child number three got "Mother Mellow," who revealed a sense of humor and admitted to mistakes from time to time. The only items in his baby book were a footprint made at the hospital and congratulations from the insurance agent.

Now the oldest child could have said, "You ruined my life by being too attentive," and the youngest could have said, "You ruined my life by not giving me enough attention." Both would have been right, yet wrong. Mother was only doing the best she knew how. She was human.

DADS AND ADULT CHILDREN

Often a retired father realizes after he stops working that he has been concentrating so hard on work over the years, or was absent from home so much while his children were growing up, he hardly even knows his own kids. He may want to get closer to his adult children, but he doesn't know how. Perhaps he believes, "I'm no good at this relationship stuff," and continues to leave relationships with his adult children to his wife, thereby cheating himself of the pleasure of knowing his children. Maybe he fears rejection, and with good reason.

Some adult children are angry with their father. I've met a few who are vengeful: "He paid no attention to me when I needed him, so why should I pay attention to him now?" But I believe they're outnumbered by young people who would love to get to know their dad better, but feel awkward around him.

The only way to break these barriers down is for you, Dad, to seek opportunities for one-on-one meetings with your son or daughter without Mom present. Invite your adult child to do something you both enjoy, whether it's a sport, meeting, breakfast, or lunch at a restaurant. If you've never hugged him or her, do it. Touch does more than words to make these special people feel loved.

HELP EACH OTHER CHANGE

And, of course, mothers have to be willing to let this happen. Since our married children live on the opposite coast, most of our communication is by phone. My husband complained that if I got on the phone extension while he was talking, the kids talked to me and shut him out. Once I realized this, I agreed that we would make separate phone calls from then on. By removing myself, I helped the children break the habit formed in childhood of communicating more easily with me than with him.

Sometimes parents are too proud to make the first overtures. I know a lot of people my age feel, "If my kids want a relationship, they'll have to come to me." They're in for a lonely old age.

Some people remain terrified of intimacy. They long to be understood, but they'd rather be lonely than take the risk of letting someone else *really* get to know them. But other people—including our own children—can empathize with us only to the extent that we let them know us.

Most of us have been brought up not fully sharing our feelings, even within our own families. Some non-threatening ways of doing this will be suggested later in this chapter.

WHAT WERE YOU LIKE AS A PARENT?

Your children were not raised by your "current self" — relatively wise, caring, and mature — but by your "young self" — inexperienced, uncertain, and nervous.

My friend Liz calls her younger self the "plastic bubble lady." She used to play the role of censor; she doesn't do that anymore. As she tells it, "My friends say, 'I can tell you things now that I couldn't in the past when you were in your plastic bubble.'"

My children were raised by my "critical parent," whose voice I had internalized. The oldest got the most of her. (Which explains, as Bombeck points out, why most parental kiss-and-tell books are written by the firstborn.) My critical parent self doesn't live here any more, but the damage she did lives on. The past can't be erased — *but* it can be healed.

It's very healing to share your struggles to change with your adult children. It gives them hope — older people don't need to remain stuck in their old ways forever. It also changes their perception of you for the better. "You're attractive to young people when they can see that you're still growing," Liz comments. "They want to be around you."

Even after parents are no longer alcoholic or abusive, many young adults are still carrying around a lot of angry baggage from their childhood. You may have hurt them deeply without meaning to. Children are sensitive. Something you said or did that you don't even remember may still be festering inside them. I believe in asking for their forgiveness. It will help them let go of some of the hurts of the past, and they really need to do that.

WE REMEMBER QUITE DIFFERENTLY

Children's memories are not always accurate. Pat's adult daughter Steffi accused her of always favoring her brother. The evidence: "You drove him to speech therapy every week for a year."

"But I drove you to dance lessons every week for three years," Pat said. "Have you forgotten that?"

Our memories are selective. We tend to edit them to fit our

present needs. In Steffi's case, it was her need to be angry at her mother. But until these feelings came out, Pat had no opportunity to talk to her about what had been between them in the past that was *still influencing their present relationship*.

One way of opening up a discussion with an adult child would be to say, "Share with me your perception of what it was like for you growing up. Was there some time when I wasn't there for you?" And then listen without interrupting and without getting defensive.

WHY BRING UP THE PAST?

Some people say, or think, "Why rake up all that garbage from the past? What's done is done."

But the problem is that it's *not* done. Because we are human, we carry our pasts around inside our heads. If the past was hurtful, we can continue to carry it around, letting it damage our present lives, or we can let it out, where we at least stand a fighting chance of taking some of the sting out of it.

Talking about the past changes the way you feel about it. You can help your adult children gain a new perspective on their childhood just by encouraging them to talk about it. Time alone with an adult child is often difficult to come by, but it can be a marvelous opportunity for healing.

Evelyn's twenty-seven-year-old daughter came home to recuperate from a broken leg. Kelly had spent a lot of time as a teenager hiding out in her room, hurt and angry. A lot of these old issues were still unresolved. Talking them out while her parents were caring for her helped her resolve them.

I have to admit, however, that it doesn't always work out this way. Another friend of mine had a daughter about the same age who came home to recuperate from severe injuries suffered in an auto accident. But her presence caused tension in the household with her mother's new husband, and nothing was resolved.

Part of the problem was that the daughter had always resented her mother's remarriage. While her mother was single, the adult children got a lot of her attention. Now her husband came first.

FOLLOWING OLD SCRIPTS

Negative, hurtful behavior can be passed down from one generation to another perpetually, unless somebody decides to say, "It stops here!" and makes a change.

Bev is the adult daughter of an alcoholic father whose binges always ruined their Christmas. She is not an alcoholic herself, but every year she follows the family script. "It's as if a timer in my head goes off," she said. "Okay, we're having too much fun here. It's time to ruin it."

The last time she did this, starting an argument in the middle of opening presents, her oldest daughter said, "Mother, this has to stop. Every year you do something like this. I don't want to pass this on to my children for the next generation."

After the shock wore off, Bev realized that her daughter was right. "Oh, honey," she said, "I don't know how to stop. Please help me." And they held each other and cried.

What would you do if one of your children confronted you like that? Would you see it as an opportunity or as a threat? If you shared with her what life was like for you as a child, would both of you have a new understanding of why you act the way you do?

SHARE YOUR MEMORIES

What if I told you that there is an almost guaranteed way to let your children get to know you better, to help them feel closer to you, and to perhaps heal old wounds, giving them a priceless gift that money can't buy that will help bind the generations together? You won't have to spend a cent for counseling—in fact, it's very low cost—and you probably already have all the tools and materials you need right at home. Does it sound too good to be true?

Sharing your memories with your children is a tried and true, although very indirect, way to accomplish all this and more. Sometimes, having serious conversations with people about relationships doesn't work. You feel self-conscious, or else they just don't want to hear it. Or you lack the communication skills.

But nobody can resist a story. Stories draw people into them in a non-threatening way. Stories can get a point across without seeming to. Moreover, stories about your early life reveal who you are in a way that your children can accept.

"The little boy or girl you once were you still are," say Kevin Leman and Randy Carlson in their book *Unlocking the Secrets of Your Childhood Memories*. This is not mere theory, say the authors, but something they see confirmed in counseling every day. This doesn't mean that you have to psychoanalyze yourself when you talk or write about the past. But it does mean that you can proceed with confidence because nothing you remember will be insignificant or trivial (although it is important to make sure that your memory reflects something that really took place). But the point is that in many ways you *are* your memories.

Doug, sixty-two, grew up during the Depression. His father was an insurance salesman whose income was erratic. Money was a constant source of anxiety. One day, when he was older, Doug's father told him about an incident he had never forgotten. He was walking down Canal Street in New York on his way to call on a client when a brick fell from a building, narrowly missing him. His first thought, he told Doug, was, "Why didn't that hit me? If I'd been killed accidentally, my wife and children would be well taken care of by my life insurance."

WE ARE OUR MEMORIES

This glimpse into his father's pain, which Doug shared with his adult children, helped them to understand his cautious approach to money and his fears about financial security.

What was it like to live through the Depression? What did you do during World War II? What was school like for you? Did you have a favorite toy?

Are your children really interested in knowing all this? Most of us have said very little about ourselves to our children. For a variety of reasons—perhaps the rise of television and the decline of family storytelling, perhaps the absence of grandparents in the home—we just haven't talked much about the past.

Sometimes adult children become keenly aware of what they're missing as they grow older. A fortyish woman who was caring for her frail mother of seventy-nine told me, "I've asked her over and over again about her early life. I wish my mother would tell me more. But she just won't." The reason for her anguish was that she was afraid her mother would soon die and she never would have really known her. This happens all too frequently.

I don't know if we realize the disservice we do our children when we refuse to let them know us. They are the heirs not only of our lives but of an entire line of ancestors. Denied access to this information, they are to some degree denied the security of knowing who they are.

THE PAST AS A TREASURE HOUSE

Perhaps it's our pioneer heritage, but Americans often view the past as something to run away from. But there is another way of looking at the past: as a treasure to be shared. Unlike money, you can give away this treasure freely and still get to keep it. Nobody can ever take it away from you.

Melvin A. Kimble, a seminary professor and gerontologist, teaches seminarians how to help aging people tell their life stories. He quotes to them a saying of Viktor Frankl: "Memory is a granary into which we've brought the harvest of our lives."

Some people are afraid to talk about childhood memories because they don't want to be reminded of their past unhappiness. You can't rewrite the past, but you can revise it by looking at it differently—as an adult rather than a child. And if you don't want to share anything, you don't have to. You are in control of whatever you reveal.

HOW TO GET STARTED

There are many ways to share your memories. You can talk into a tape recorder; you can have someone videotape you; or you can write your story. This isn't something that has to be completed quickly. It could be an ongoing project over a long period of time.

However, this is a project that few people, no matter how well-intentioned, can complete alone. If you're recording on videotape, you'll need someone to do the filming. An "interviewer" to prime you with questions may be helpful. (Husbands and wives could do this for each other.)

If you decide to write, many communities have courses available for older adults in writing their life stories. Elderhostels and churches also have started this kind of course. The group activity helps to "prime the pump" and motivate you to keep going.

Joan Hodgkin has taught a course in her community for several years called "Capture Your Memories." She takes groups of no more than fifteen people through a year of weekly classes. The object is to produce a book, along with pictures. But many people take the class over two or three times because it's so much fun.

"This is not therapy and it's not a creative writing class," Joan says. "I give them some basics, such as, 'Write about how you felt; don't just give the facts,' but I don't critique the writing."

She points out, "They're not writing for publication. They're writing for themselves. One person's memory will trigger another and they ricochet back and forth. If they come up against sensitive material and they can't write through it, which I encourage, I tell them to just skip it."

What will trigger memories and help you get started?

Interview your parents and other family members. This will fill in gaps in your knowledge and give you some additional insight.

Look at old photos. They never fail to bring back memories.

Draw a diagram of the house you grew up in. Walk yourself through the rooms in your own mind, picturing things that happened there.

Look at old newspapers and magazines. What was going on in the world? What were you doing when all this happened?

Take a thematic approach. What do you remember about childhood foods, clothing, friends, relatives, teachers, school, vacations, the old neighborhood, or the farm you grew up on?

Be sure to bring the story up to the present. Your children need to know what it feels like to grow older. As your story moves forward and encompasses their lives, they have another source against which to check their memories.

Recently, there's been an explosion of resources developed to encourage reminiscence. Many of these have been designed for use with extremely elderly people in nursing home settings. If your parents are still living, I would certainly encourage you to use these aids to help them come to terms with their own lives, one of the major spiritual tasks of old age.

But there's no reason why you couldn't use these same books and games to help you tell your life story to your adult children and grandchildren.

QUESTIONS FOR DISCUSSION

Use the following topics and suggestions to write or tell at least one other person some of the memorable details of your own life. Remember to include not only the facts but also how you felt about what happened to you.[1]

Birth to Five Years

- Parents (brief history).
- Full names, birth dates, marriage dates, death dates, immigration records (if applicable).
- Your birth: when, where, circumstances, etc.
- Description of your mother: physical characteristics, personality, talents, temperament, family stories about her, her role in the home.
- Description of your father: (same as above).
- Brothers and sisters: names, birth dates, characteristics, personalities, talents, roles in the home.
- Earliest memories of grandparents: names, birthplaces, histories (if known), personalities, talents, customs or traditions, languages spoken, memories of their homes, family heirlooms from them, etc.
- Earliest childhood memories.

Ages Five to Twelve

- Description of house or houses you lived in, neighborhood, neighbors.
- Community: characteristics of town, city, farm where you lived, important buildings, economic activities, traditions, population, etc.
- Medical: experience with doctors, dentists, childhood diseases or epidemics.
- School days: names of schools attended, special teachers, good or bad experiences, school friends, special activities, influences important to you later on.
- Relatives.
- Animals and pets.
- Games and entertainment.
- Favorite sayings, songs, rhymes, poems, ditties, etc.
- Fads: movies, box tops, radio programs, heroes.
- Favorite clothing.
- Hobbies.
- Jobs or chores.
- Family life: fun times together, family projects, vacations,

shopping, financial conditions.

- Family difficulties: sickness and grievances, accidents, operations, death of loved ones.
- Spiritual life practiced in the home: faith-promoting stories.
- Exciting experiences: scouts, friends, church outings, etc.
- Additional information: unusual happenings or visitors; events that changed your life.

Ages Thirteen to Nineteen

- Your personality, dreams, and goals.
- High school: courses and achievements, activities, sports and clubs, influential teachers and friends, important decisions, escapades.
- Social life: dances, movies, dating.
- Talents and hobbies.
- Jobs and work experiences.
- Religious practice and experiences.
- Early romances.
- Signs of the times: what was going on in the world, national and world events, sports, music, entertainment, etc.

Early Adult Life

- Military service and experiences (if any).
- College or technical school: school attended and why selected, special friends, influential teachers and courses, social life, etc.
- Courtship and marriage: how you met, special dates, marriage plans, meeting in-laws for first time, mate's personality, details of your wedding (where, when, attendants, etc.).
- Married life: settling down, making ends meet, marital adjustments, spats, etc.
- Vocation: career and how selected, changes, promotions, job transfers, successes and failures, unusual job experiences.
- Children: names and birth dates, personalities and characteristics, humorous episodes, joys and problems, etc.
- Child-rearing philosophy.
- Religious practices in the home.
- Family traditions.
- Family vacations.

CHAPTER FIFTEEN

BEING THERE FOR YOUR GRANDCHILDREN

"If I'd known it was going to be this much fun, I'd have had my grandchildren first."
Anonymous Grandmother

Often new grandparents are surprised by the depth of their feelings, so different from the feelings we have for our children. "I held my first grandchild when he was newborn, and stared and stared at him," Ethel said. "I couldn't seem to get enough of him."

Like falling in love, grandparenthood is hard to put into words. You have to experience it. This tiny baby is our connection to a future we'll never know. "Awesome," as the kids say.

Arthur Kornhaber, M.D., who was one of the first to speak out about the feelings of today's grandparents and their grandchildren, says, "The connection between grandparents and grandchild is natural and second in emotional power only to the primordial bond between parent and child."[1]

WHY GRANDPARENTS ARE IMPORTANT

Except for making us feel good, why do we need our grandchildren and why do they need us? Research points to grandparents as important forces in the lives of grandchildren, say Vern L. Bengtson and Joan F. Robertson in their book *Grandparenthood*, but it's difficult to say exactly what grandparents do. The authors conclude that whatever they do is not nearly as important as their simply being there. By their presence, grandparents:

- *Support their children's transition into parenthood.* Grandmothers, especially, act as "stabilizers" of mothers, resulting in greater maternal warmth and competence.
- *Soften the intensity of modern family life, moderating conflicts.* Grandparents do this chiefly by giving both generations "a place to go," that is, a safety valve.
- *Carry and interpret family history and traditions for the grandchildren.* This connection with their past gives children a secure foundation from which to launch into the future.

In addition, grandchildren can be a powerful force bringing the generations together. Parents feel a new appreciation for *their* parents, and a desire to get closer to them. Grandparents feel a new respect for and gratitude to their children. I recall that my two older children reached a new status in my eyes. They were now the mother and father of my grandchildren!

WHAT CHILDREN GET FROM GRANDPARENTS

Good grandparents give a child *unconditional love* (unlike parents, who are always asking you to "do things").

Today's parents tend to push children too hard, "hurrying them through childhood as if it were a waste of time," says child psychologist and author Eda LeShan. "Grandparents are needed for a sensible balance" to the "horrendous academic pressures" and "impossible expectations on the playing fields."[2]

Having people who are crazy about him just because he exists is a powerful boost to any child's self-esteem. Conversely, if grandparents are harsh, critical, or distant, the child suffers.

Dr. Arthur Kornhaber, a child psychiatrist, and his wife, Carol, interviewed hundreds of grandchildren. Of those grandchildren whose grandparents were not a part of their lives, some concluded sadly, "I guess I'm not good enough. They don't like me."

Children who have close grandparents turn out to be more emotionally secure. Also, grandparents teach children to love and respect old people. Research has shown that people who did not know their grandparents when they were growing up are more likely to dislike and fear old people.

AS OLD AS GOD?

Grandparents are mentors, introducing the child to a larger world beyond their home. Their importance as *spiritual* mentors cannot be overestimated. "Grandpa is so old," little children reason, "he must be almost as old as God." Therefore, in the eyes of young children, grandparents know all about God and can act as trustworthy guides to what God is like.

"God's love is like a grandparents'," says Richard L. Morgan in his devotional book *No Wrinkles on the Soul*. Grandparents love children before they're born, just as God has loved us from all eternity.

To the child, says Kornhaber, a grandparent is "hero, wizard and crony."[3] Their tales from the past make grandparents seem larger-than-life figures in the child's eyes. A grandparent removing his dentures seems magical, dwelling in a strange, wonderful world. He can do anything!

As a crony, a grandparent hangs out with the child and sometimes does things with him that the parent wouldn't allow. This alliance with the child against parental authority can make the child crazy about a grandparent and make parents crazy. "Sometimes I feel like I'm dealing with two sets of children," a parent once sighed.

WHAT DO GRANDPARENTS GET OUT OF THE ROLE?

If not overdone, the typical crony role with children is good for grandparents. It helps us get in touch with the long-lost "child within," which is often the most creative and fun part of our personalities.

Grandchildren, besides making grandparents feel young again, give them a future, an assurance that the family line will be carried on. They contribute to the grandparents' self-esteem. It feels good to be able to contribute to the child's welfare, to be an influence for good in a young life.

Since most modern grandparents are active people, theirs can be the pleasure of introducing the child to a wide range of experiences. A grandmother who became an actress late in life takes her grandchildren to watch commercials being filmed. A grandfather who is a devoted outdoorsman takes his grandson river rafting. Grandchildren give grandparents the opportunity to make memories neither of them will ever forget.

But for many, the greatest joy of grandparenthood by far is the joy of the "second chance." If there were things you missed out doing with your own kids, life has given you another opportunity to do them at last.

WHAT KINDS OF GRANDPARENTS ARE THERE?

If you had a loving relationship with a grandparent, you will be eager to be a good grandparent, too. But you may fear it's impossible because you're comparing yourself to a type of grandparent you will never be: the quaint, domestic grandmother bustling about making cookies, or the humorous, cuddly grandfather puttering in the workshop. Our grandparents had almost no interests outside their homes and families, but few modern grandparents are rocking chair types.

Not knowing how to act leaves us feeling awkward and unsure of ourselves in the grandparenting role. Fortunately, those little kids in front of you are new at being grandchildren, too. And remember that there is more than one way to be a grandparent. Researchers have identified the following "styles" of grandparenting:

The formal. This type follows "proper" procedures and is not overly indulgent with the children. He or she is careful not to offer advice, or to overstep the bounds. This formal grandparent expects to be treated with respect, and tends to emphasize good manners.

The fun seeker. This type of grandparent joins the child in fun activities. The lines of authority are irrelevant. Fun seekers may invite the child to join them (for example, in a trip to Disney World), or they may join in the child's play. My father was a fun seeker type of grandparent, always down on the floor playing with my children when they were little and joining in their games. My mother was more formal.

The distant figure. This grandparent emerges only on holidays and ritual occasions. Contact with the grandchildren is fleeting and infrequent.

The surrogate parent. This is usually a grandparent who is taking care of a child when both parents must work. However, for the approximately 5 percent of the children in this country who live with their grandparents, grandparents may be the only parents they know.

The reservoir of family wisdom. This is an authority figure, usually a grandfather, who is considered the patriarch of a large, extended family. Everybody seeks his counsel.

The influential. These grandparents are very much involved in the grandchildren's lives, almost as influential as parents without becoming surrogate parents.

Ellen is almost always available to babysit her grandchildren. She takes great delight in having them around. When the parents are away, Ellen and Charles have them for days and weeks at a time.

"Don't you ever find them a burden?" I asked.

"Sometimes. I used to dread all the work and feel, 'Do I have to do this?' But I made a conscious decision to make my grandchildren my 'ministry.' I want my life to count in my grandchildren's lives. I asked the Lord, 'What can I do to make memories and be an influence for good?' That changed my entire outlook," Ellen said.

Ellen didn't have a grandmother in her life when she was a child. She used her mother's grandmothering as a model for the role, as well as the style of some of her older friends.

But it's impossible to be an "influential" grandparent without frequent contact with the grandchildren. It demands a commitment of time, energy, even money that many grandparents are unable or unwilling to provide. Many grandparents just live too far away. They may still have full-time jobs and lack the time, or they may feel that they are now entitled to have time for themselves at last.

Many of the people who are grandparents today have been influenced by the all-pervasive human potential movement in the United States. Their theme song is "I Gotta Be Me." The majority of middle-class grandparents studied in one research sample were either "fun seekers" or "distant figures." Some distant figures lived in the same town as their grandchildren but seldom saw them.

THE "NEW SOCIAL CONTRACT"

The most common complaint of adult children used to be that their parents "interfered" in the raising of children. Today, the most common complaint is that the grandparents are unavailable.

Why have grandparents seemed to change so much in one short generation?

According to Dr. Kornhaber, this is the result of a "new social contract" between parents and children. The "old social contract" among extended family members assumed that attachments were lifelong and that help was passed up and down the generational ladder. But according to a new way of thinking that now prevails, emotional attachments between generations are unnecessary. We all have to be free to do our own thing. Each generation should get its emotional needs taken care of by its own age group.

But in a society of independent, age-segregated individualists, there's no commitment to the nurture of children. Children are feeling abandoned because, as Dr. Kornhaber puts it, "The brutal fact is that more and more grandparents are choosing to ignore their grandchildren."[4] Commonly heard remarks such as "I've paid my dues" and "Now it's their turn" are used to justify this behavior.

Unlike traditional societies, our society provides no "common ground" on which extended families can unite. Families have to build their own bridges through family interaction.[5] Becoming part of your grandchildren's lives is not going to just happen. It's going to take a conscious decision and a lot of effort on your part to make it happen. Along the way, there are many obstacles to overcome.

OBSTACLES TO GRANDPARENTING

Besides physical distance, the biggest obstacle to closeness with grandchildren is the same as it's always been: intergenerational feuding. The arrival of a grandchild is a powerful motivation to make peace, but not all families reunite. Instead, they may find they have something new to fight about, as well as a new weapon to use against each other: the grandchildren.

However, with the arrival of grandchildren, the power balance in the family begins to tip in the direction of your children. They can now decide when—and even if—you can see the grandchildren. If the parents are divorced, the custodial parent will sometimes deny you the right to see your own grandchildren. If either parent feels you've injured them and they are vindictive, they now have a way of getting even, and there is little you can do about it.

Until recently, grandparents had no legal right to have access to their grandchildren. Some states now grant such rights (but not automatically) in case of death or divorce. A few others allow you to petition the court for visitation rights even when the parents are not divorced. But it's an ugly business. You may drag the child through a traumatic and expensive court procedure and still lose. Even if you win, you may lose. Once a month court-mandated visits under the eyes of a hostile parent may not be much fun for either generation.

Of course, denying the children their grandparents can backfire on parents. I will never forget an adult student in one of my writing classes who couldn't forgive her parents for cutting off contact with her beloved grandmother when she was a child. The hurt from that loss was as fresh as if it had happened yesterday. The grandmother was dead and gone, but the parents had lost their child's heart by their cruelty.

DANGER TO THE CHILDREN

Parents may feel that some of the older generation's habits could endanger the children. If you smoke, parents may not want their children to stay in your home where they'll be exposed to secondhand smoke, a proven health hazard. If one of the grandparents is an alcoholic, the danger of alcohol-related accidents or abuse of the child is not something that parents can just ignore.

Al and Marge are recovering alcoholics in their sixties. They were doing very well until a business reversal plunged their affluent lives into chaos. "A glass of wine or two just to relax is okay," they thought. "We can handle it." But when their son said, "I can't let the children come over when we're not there unless you stop drinking," they stopped.

Another danger that parents worry about is child abuse or molestation. If the parents believe that there is a possibility this could happen, they may not allow you to see the child alone. Whether or not their concern is justified, this is a point of potential contention if they question your approach to discipline, etc.

AREAS OF CONFLICT

What are some of the other reasons why grandparent-grandchildren relationships can cause conflict with the parents?

Jealousy on the part of the parents. Sometimes this is jealousy of you, due to the fact that the parents fear the child will love you more than he does them. Sometimes this is jealousy of their own children ("How come you never did all this for me?").

A little tact on your part will go a long way toward alleviating this tension. Is the jealous parent insecure, or have you been badmouthing the parent or encouraging the child to rebel against parental authority? There's a lot you can do to boost a parent's power and prestige in the child's eyes and to encourage a child to "do something nice for Daddy" or "buy something for Mommy to surprise her."

Do you focus all your attention on the grandchild and ignore or belittle your own children? Many young people of our children's generation feel unloved by their parents. "What! After all we gave them, after all we did for them?" Yes, but they never really *felt* what we were doing as love. They never got our approval or blessing in the way they would have liked. Now they have to watch their children getting the love they may feel is rightfully theirs.

The only solution is to build the one-on-one relationship with your child. Your support and approval will make him or her a better parent and indirectly benefit the grandchild.

Coming on too strong. Grandparents can get really pushy, overwhelming young parents with advice and the grandchildren with gifts. Sometimes this happens because they are competing with the other set of grandparents. Too much attention and too many gifts will make your children feel powerless and your grandchildren selfish, greedy, and manipulative. Back off a bit. Your time and attention are much better for the grandchildren than material things.

Undermining the parents' discipline. You may not agree with the way your children discipline your grandchildren, but unless they are being abusive, it's their right to choose their own parenting style and enforce their own rules. If children know that when Mommy and Daddy say no, they can always get what they want from Grandma or Grandpa, your children will be justifiably angry.

Child-rearing practices are an enormous bone of contention in families because they seem to reverse themselves every generation, oscillating between extremes of strictness and permissiveness. As a result, each generation is busy correcting the previous generation's mistakes.

You can best help your grandchildren's parents not by criticizing and correcting their methods of discipline, but by encouraging them to heal the relationship with you. A lot of problems that parents have with children stem from their own childhood.

I make it clear that when I'm babysitting, I'll use the methods that seem best to me, while at the same time acknowledging the rules and parameters established by my grandchildren's parents. I've observed that children don't feel the need to test their grandparents the way they test their parents. Still, we must remember to give room for the personal dynamics between children and parents. It used to drive me crazy that my kids behaved so much better with my parents than they did with me, but my grandkids seem to be following the same pattern.

SOME PARENTS EXPECT TOO MUCH

Baby boomers were some of the most overindulged children in history, and some of them still expect their parents to be at their beck and call.

Nancy's daughter Shelley and her husband, Lee, expected her to quit her part-time job and babysit her grandbaby so that Shelley could go back to work. Nancy was quite willing to help in an emergency, but she was not willing to raise her daughter's baby for her. At first, the young parents were very angry at Nancy's refusal, but they got over it.

Young parents may not understand that you don't have the same energy at sixty as you did at thirty. You may have health problems. You may have other responsibilities, such as an ill spouse or an aging parent to care for, which leave you physically and emotionally drained. Your children won't realize this unless you tell them. Even so, they may not want to hear this because they don't want to believe you're getting older.

But don't blame them if you feel put upon. It's up to *you* to decide how much of a commitment of your time and energy you can make to grandparenting in retirement and to set limits and make them known to your children.

TODAY'S CHILDREN ARE DIFFERENT

In many ways, today's kids are different. If they watch television, they may be exposed to more sex and violence in a week than we heard about in a lifetime. They're more aware of dangers, more anxious, more vulnerable to peer pressure. They live in a more dangerous world than our children did.

We used to let our kids roam freely in our suburban neighborhoods. Today, in the suburbs of large cities, parents worry about kidnaping and child molestation. Children are watched more closely and given less freedom. Grandparents need to understand these pressures on parents and children, and not compare their grandchildren with their own children at the same age.

Grandparents sometimes have difficulty with the present younger generation's openness. We weren't allowed to talk like that to grownups! But children *can* learn to express their feelings without being disrespectful, and grandparents can tactfully help them learn this. Sometimes children who have emotional problems "act out" their pain and distress, and can get totally out of control. Grandparents who give them extra love and attention can help a lot, but it won't be easy.

OUR SKILLS ARE RUSTY

It's been a long time since most of us have been around babies and young children, but we can learn. There are even courses in some communities on "how to grandparent." You can review what kids need at various ages and how to meet their needs for loving support. You can also learn new ways of disciplining that work better than some of your old methods. I've learned a lot from my adult children that I wish I'd known when they were little.

Sometimes parents are afraid the grandparents will indoctrinate the children in beliefs that they don't approve of. If there are religious differences, grandparents ought not to get too pushy. Ask if it's all right to take children to your religious services. Show respect for what the parents are teaching, even if you don't agree with it. Nobody can stop you from praying for your grandchildren or from living a life that exemplifies what you believe. One great privilege of being a grandparent is taking little children in your arms and praying for them.

Occasionally, grandchildren become a bone of contention in a post-retirement marriage. A retired couple will differ about the amount of involvement to have with the grandchildren. Usually, it's Grandma who wants the grandkids around a lot and Grandpa who complains about them. Compromises are in order.

How about letting Grandma babysit in the children's home instead of yours, or have them over when Grandpa is doing something else away from the house? Or better yet, both Grandpa and Grandma can have the fun of getting better acquainted with each child by going one-on-one with them instead of seeing grandkids in gangs.

TAKE THE INITIATIVE

To receive your grandkids' love and respect, you have to invest time and energy in them, say authors and grandparents Spike and Darnell White. Build a *direct* relationship with each child. Don't relate to the grandchildren only through their parents, or rely only on the parents' secondhand reports. As soon as they're old enough, give the children your phone number and invite them to call collect when they want to talk to you. And don't wait to be invited to see your grandchildren or wait for the parents to call you first.

Darnell says, "There are times when we feel neglected and think our children don't care about us. Don't sit there depressed, waiting for the phone to ring. When you want to hear from them, *you* call them. . . . I invite the family (one or all) over for dinner, a picnic, cake or pie, cookies, cinnamon rolls, just anything. I encourage you—take the initiative!"

"In this push and pull world we live in," say Spike and Darnell, "providing grandchildren with the opportunity to be quiescent is a special privilege grandparents can offer."[6] In other words, don't feel you have to be constantly entertaining them.

Sometimes Ruth and Jack have trouble knowing what to do with Ruth's oldest grandson, Mark. Mark is used to traveling with his well-to-do parents, staying at the best hotels and eating in fancy restaurants. But when the grandparents suggest something different, such as a picnic, he's quite happy with that.

"Maybe the best thing you and Jack are doing for Mark," I suggested to Ruth, "is teaching him that it's possible to have fun without spending a lot of money."

WHAT IF THERE IS CHILD ABUSE?

There is one unpleasant subject that was usually ignored in the past, but we cannot close our eyes to it. If you become aware that your grandchildren are being physically or sexually abused, it is your duty to protect them. You need to be very sure of your accusations, however, before you report child abuse. If the parents are exonerated, you will lose both your children *and* your grandchildren. If the parents are found guilty, you may need to be prepared to step in and help care for the children, or else they will probably be removed from the home and placed in foster care.

The biographies of adults who were abused as children testify to the importance of grandparents. Even when the grandparents didn't take over their care, the mere existence of grandparents who loved them helped them to endure their difficult childhood. And the memories of this love helped to heal them as adults.

If the parents divorce, grandparents are extremely important in providing a safe harbor to help the grandchildren ride out the storm. "What can a pair of sixty-five-year-olds do to comfort and reassure the innocent victims of the Me Generation's hedonism and self-absorption?" wondered Bev Shaver when her eight- and eleven-year-old granddaughters came to visit after their parents decided to divorce.

The most important thing the Shavers did was to put aside their own anger, listen to the children, and reassure them that the breakup was not their fault. Just by being people they can count on, grandparents give the children hope. They can't "kiss and make it better" for the children after the divorce, but they can help to make it bearable.

"UNPLANNED PARENTHOOD"

Almost none of the millions of retirees who have become parents of their grandchildren expected to be raising children again at their age. Some of these grandchildren are the children of drug-addicted parents. If it weren't for the grandparents, these neglected children would become wards of the state. Some of these children were born addicted, and many have serious physical and mental problems. They are not easy children to care for, and in many locales, grandparents get no child support.

They could be your neighbors, like Leah and Dan, who have had Leah's grandson, Josh, now eleven, living with them since he was eight years old. Shortly before that, his parents were divorced.

His father moved away and his mother took off for weeks at a time, leaving the boy with her mother and stepfather.

Finally, in order to give the boy's life some stability, Leah agreed to take him until her daughter could get her life together. "But I don't think that's ever going to happen," Leah said. "We have total physical, emotional, and financial responsibility."

It hasn't been easy. The pain of his abandonment made Josh an angry and disruptive child. The first year they had him, Leah got almost daily calls from school. Now, she said proudly, they've gone an entire year since he was sent to the principal's office.

"When he's home, he requires constant attention and reinforcement," Leah said. "But we can see the progress. His teacher told us, 'If this kid makes it, it will be because of what you two have done.'"

Leah admits, "There's a lot we don't do. We don't do Scouts. We don't do Little League. But we give his life structure and stability, which he needs badly."

Leah has had to cut back sharply on her work and her commitment to outside organizations. They need the income from Dan's job, so retirement is out of the question for as long as they are raising Josh. Fortunately, "Dan is so easygoing," Leah said. "He has much more patience than I do. I couldn't handle Josh by myself."

Leah and Dan recognize the boy's vulnerability, dependency, and anxiety. "He worries about us," Leah says. "We can't get sick. If I have the flu, or if I'm late getting home and I'm not there when he comes home from school, he gets very upset."

This is not carefree, happy grandparenthood they're experiencing. Grandparents who are parents have little in common with other grandparents their own age, and feel out of place with young parents. But they are not alone. There are a few organizations that try to help.

The reward for Leah and Dan, as with all grandparents, is to see that they have made a major difference in shaping the life and welfare of their own family that will continue long after them.

QUESTIONS FOR DISCUSSION

1. Do you have grandchildren? Do you feel close to them? Why, or why not?

2. If you are not satisfied with your relationships with grandchildren, what action can you take?
3. Do you and your spouse agree on the amount of time, money, etc., that you will spend on grandchildren?
4. How can you support each other in becoming better grandparents?

CHAPTER SIXTEEN

THE CHALLENGE OF LONG-DISTANCE GRANDPARENTING

You are important in the recipe of building your grandkids' lives – and don't ever think you aren't!
Darnell White

How can you be important to your grandchildren if you live too far away to see them frequently? Is a relationship with them beyond your grasp?

It's easy to give in to the temptation to just give up. It will take real effort and motivation to counteract that sense of futility and get moving. You may have to rearrange some of your priorities. You may have to change some of your habits. But keeping in touch at a distance *is* possible.

What matters is our *availability* and our *consistency*. Children have to know that we are always available to listen to them. In order for them to feel this way, we have to make contact with them on a regular basis.

This means regular phone calls – weekly, if possible – made directly to each grandchild, and letters, also addressed directly to the child. Even before they can read, children love to get mail. Letters don't have to be long; in fact, shorter is better. And they have the advantage of lasting – they can be kept and reread.

What do you say during phone calls?

It's probably better to do more listening than talking. Most grandkids like to chatter. But you do need to talk about what the kids are interested in, which changes constantly. It also helps to remember (or relearn) the various developmental stages that children go through. If your grandchild likes a particular television show or movie, you watch it, too, so you'll have something in common to talk about.

What are his interests? Clip articles and cartoons about his favorite things and send these with your letters.

Enclose little surprises in your letters: a stick of gum, money to buy an ice cream cone, a picture to color, a inexpensive toy or trinket, stickers, etc.

GRANDPARENTS AS STORYTELLERS

Tell riddles, jokes, and stories. You don't know any? Go to the library and get out some books. Learn some.

In the last ten years, there has been a renaissance in storytelling. Professional storytellers from every ethnic group perform regularly. Audio tapes of professional storytellers are widely available. Stories from your ethnic background will enrich a grandchild's life and give him a sense of "belonging." (A children's librarian can help you find collections of ethnic stories.)

While reading to a child is invaluable, so is the spoken or "told" story. Recently, I attended a workshop in my community given by a professional storyteller to help people gain some storytelling skills. Most of the attendees were schoolteachers and librarians, but two were grandmas who were there to learn to improve their storytelling to grandchildren.

If you'd like a few pointers on storytelling, I'd recommend the following books available from the National Association for the Preservation and Perpetuation of Storytelling: *The Family Storytelling Handbook* by Anne Pellowski, *Just Enough to Make a Story* by Nancy Schimmel, and *From Wonder to Wisdom: Using Stories to Help Children Grow* by Charles A. Smith.

By all means, read or tell Bible stories to your grandchildren. There's a wealth of Bible story books for children, but you might also consider telling some of these stories from memory. For some pointers on memorizing and bringing these stories to life for all ages, consult Thomas E. Boomershine's *Story Journey: An Invitation to the Gospel as Storytelling*, also available from the NAPPS.

READING ON TAPE

What I do—and I don't remember where I got this idea—is record myself reading the book to the child on tape, then mail both the book and the tape. You don't always have to buy and send the book; you can also read library books.

You can also pass on stories from your family's history on tape. Children love stories of what their parents were doing when they were children.

Also, tell stories of your own childhood. My husband and I started something we call "The Grandparent Tapes" on audio cassettes. The first one was about toys and games we remember from childhood. Others in the series are foods, friends, relatives, our childhood neighborhoods, school days, etc. Making the tapes together, we "interviewed" each other, asking each other questions. Each of us stimulated the other's memories. If you have a camcorder, this could just as well be done on video.

OTHER IDEAS

Some other ideas for long-distance grandparents, culled from a variety of sources:

If you saved pictures from your children's childhood—their drawings, report cards, whatever—you can send a photo or drawing in each letter with a story tape.

Many families exchange videotapes. Why not videotape yourself reading or telling a story? One enterprising grandma thought her very young grandchildren would relate better to the videotape if there were children in it. So she had herself taped reading stories to a group of neighborhood kids.

Do you ever send food? Cookies are always a big hit. But perhaps you could make and send traditional foods of your family's ethnic group to the grandchildren.

Start a family newsletter or round-robin letter. Have everybody contribute a recipe, drawing, story, or poem, make copies, and then send them to all family members, including children.

Send the grandchildren a supply of stamped, self-addressed envelopes and ask them to send you some of their work regularly— a school paper, drawing, story, or whatever they like. Start a file for each grandchild and save these papers.

IDEAS FOR VISITS

When you see grandchildren infrequently, it's easy to get carried away—you expect too much, do too much, spend too much—and so there is potential for everybody to come away disappointed. Short visits are best. Make them want more not less of you.

"Sometimes we try to do too much," my friend Helen said. "One day, I had a big day planned with the grandkids. We were going to go swimming, and then I was going to take them into the city to eat. After we went swimming, we were all hot and tired and they said, 'Do we have to go into the city? Can't we just go to your house and play?' So we did."

When grandkids visit, let them help you—in the garden, in the workshop, in the kitchen. Cook or garden together. Make something together.

Invest in a few simple toys, crayons and paper, modeling clay, puzzles, etc. I went to garage sales and bought some basic, inexpensive toys and games for various ages that I keep just for grandkids' visits.

It's important to make holidays special. Every family has its own holiday traditions—the foods and rituals that children will remember all their lives. Tell grandchildren the stories behind these traditions. Don't forget: You're making memories.

Provide "a place to be" for summer, Christmas, or Easter school holidays. This could be your own home, your vacation cabin, or a place you rent (if you can afford it). Do the grandkids wear you out? One loving but tired grandma hired a teenage assistant for the summer to help her with the grandchildren.

INTERGENERATIONAL TRAVEL

Travel agencies are now offering a variety of escorted tours and vacation packages designed for grandparents and grandchildren together. The advantage of the group package is that grandchildren have others their own age to play with, and grandparents don't feel out of place amid a crowd of young parents. But you don't have to join a formal tour. Plan your own trip and take the grandkids. Widowed grandparents have found that a grandchild can be a great travel companion.

There are even intergenerational summer camps. One of these is run by the Foundation for Grandparenting, founded by Dr. Kornhaber, every summer in the Adirondacks. Grandparents and grandchildren bunk and eat together. They share some activities, and separate for others. There are now also one or two intergenerational Elderhostels.

SPREAD THE LOVE AROUND

Many people our age will not have grandchildren of their own or will live far away from them. Yet the world needs more grandparents, and older people need contact with children. So why not play the grandparent role for other children, too?

When we lived in Florida, an older couple in our church took the children of single parents under their wing. Whenever they could, they invited them to come along with their grandchildren and become part of the family for the day.

Grandmas and grandpas can rock the babies in a church nursery or sick babies in a hospital nursery. We can read to toddlers in Sunday schools. We can help in children's day-care centers, or become either paid workers or volunteers in other settings where children need love.

We can help at a school, scout troop, or church organization. With so many working parents, there's a real shortage of volunteers. Many children need the love that only people our age can give.

QUESTIONS FOR DISCUSSION

1. What ideas from this chapter can you use or adapt for your long-distance grandparenting?
2. Have you looked into any opportunities for volunteering with children?

PART FOUR

HOW NOT TO OUTLIVE YOUR MONEY

CHAPTER SEVENTEEN

WHAT YOU CAN'T AFFORD NOT TO KNOW

A prudent man sees danger and takes refuge,
but the simple keep going and suffer for it.
Solomon, Proverbs 22:3

In the early chapters of this book, I gave you the good news: You're probably going to live to spend twenty years or more in retirement. Now comes the bad news: The same society that expects you to live so long as a retiree also says to you, "Whatever money you have now has to last you the rest of your life. You can't earn any more, and if you do, we'll deduct part of those earnings from your Social Security payments."

What should we plan for? Fifteen years? Twenty? Thirty? Inflation? Recession? High interest rates? Low interest rates? How can anyone plan for economic conditions twenty years away when economists can't say with certainty what will happen next week?

Within the past twenty years, the United States has experienced double-digit inflation and high interest rates, then a drop in both of over 60 percent. The stock market has yo-yoed up and down. Tax laws have changed every two to three years. New financial products, some very aggressively marketed, are a constant challenge to understand and evaluate. With something this complex it's hard to know where to begin.

FOUR CHALLENGES RETIREES FACE

One place we might begin is with four challenges that everybody faces at retirement, whether you realize it or not:

- Having enough income to provide for day-to-day needs.
- Protecting yourself against loss of purchasing power due to inflation.
- Providing for the future needs of a surviving spouse.
- Providing, if possible, for the possible long-term care needs of yourself and your spouse.
- Protecting your nest egg, as far as humanly possible, from economic loss, and from someone else's fraud and mismanagement.

In order to meet these challenges, you will need more expert advice than I can give you. All I can do in this brief space is introduce some topics that you need to consider very carefully. In order to formulate and carry out a financial plan for your retirement, you may need the help of an accountant for tax advice, an estate planning attorney, a financial planner, or an expert on elder law. Please remember that information goes out of date very quickly. Laws and regulations change, new conditions and new knowledge come along. Take no action based on what you read here (or anywhere else) without checking it either with the appropriate authorities (the Social Security Administration, your company's Human Resources Department, etc.) or with honest, qualified professionals.

WHERE WILL THE MONEY COME FROM?

Let's start with the first challenge, because it's also the simplest to understand: figuring out what your income will be, and making it go as far as possible.

Retirement planners often refer to the "three-legged stool" of retirement income. One of the legs of the stool is Social Security benefits for retired or disabled workers and their spouses; the second is a pension from your employer; and the third is income from whatever assets you have saved over the years, such as your house and car, savings accounts, certificates of deposit, stocks, bonds, etc.

SOCIAL SECURITY

Your Social Security income, for which you've paid all your working life, will be proportionate to your earnings. The higher your income, the higher your benefits. You can begin collecting benefits at age sixty-two, but if you do, the monthly payments will be less than if you had waited until age sixty-five. If your spouse also earned enough income to qualify, he or she can choose to take his or her own benefits *or* benefits based on your earnings, whichever is greater. If you are divorced and over sixty-two, you are entitled to benefits if your marriage lasted ten years or longer.

You can find out what your benefits will be by picking up a copy of form SSA 7004, "Request for Earnings and Benefit Estimate Statement," at your local Social Security office (or call the 800 number listed in your telephone directory, and they will mail you form SSA 7004). When you fill this out and send it in, the Social Security Administration consults its computerized account of your earnings history and sends you a statement of what your estimated monthly benefits will be. (The closer you are to retirement, the more accurate the estimate.)

Even if you think you are not eligible for Social Security, it will be worth your while to send in this form. You may have more credits than you thought. Or you may be so close to qualifying that you could work for a short time at a part-time job in order to earn enough credits to qualify.

You'll find that the amount you will get is not too impressive. Social Security was never meant to be a retiree's sole means of financial support. It's intended to supplement other retirement income. However, one advantage of these benefits is that they will go up in the future to reflect increased costs of living (COLAs, or Cost of Living Adjustments).

THE PENALTY FOR WORKING

If your Social Security income is inadequate and you must work, the benefits you receive will be reduced if you earn more than $7,080 per year when you're under age sixty-five and more than $9,720 per year from ages sixty-five to sixty-nine (1991 maximum earning figures). After reaching that amount, you lose $1 of your Social Security benefits for each $2 you earn until you're sixty-five, and $1 for each $3 you earn above the maximum from ages sixty-five to sixty-nine. After age seventy, there is no penalty for working. This applies only to earnings, *not* to investment income.

You will pay no income tax on these benefits unless your adjusted gross income plus one-half of your Social Security benefits adds up to $25,000 or more ($32,000 for a couple). These are 1991 figures; future amounts will be adjusted for inflation.

Other benefits administered by the SSA include survivors' benefits, disability benefits, Supplemental Security Income (SSI) for very low-income older, blind, and disabled persons, and Medicare, which is federal health insurance for persons over sixty-five.

There is much more that you will need to know, including when and how to apply for benefits and what documents you will need. The Social Security Administration's pamphlet entitled *Understanding Social Security* (SSA publication no. 05-10024) is available free at any Social Security office.

PRIVATE PENSIONS

If you are covered by a private pension plan, you are indeed fortunate. Only half of U.S. workers are.

The best source of information about your benefits is your company's human resources department. Will you receive a monthly payment for life? Or will you receive a lump sum that you must invest and manage yourself? In the latter case, you may need the help of a financial planner. (Investment is covered in the next chapter.)

There are additional facts that you ought to be aware of about private pensions:

- Some companies have "integrated" pension plans that reduce the benefits they pay by the amount of Social Security the worker receives. Your total under these plans may be less than you thought it would be.
- Hardly any private pension plan is indexed to the cost of living. Thus, if the cost of living goes up (as it has in the past), the amount of your pension remains the same. This means that inflation will steadily reduce the value of your pension income.
- You may be given "pay out" options at retirement time. The options that you choose will have tax consequences. If you choose to roll over your nest egg into an IRA, taxes are deferred until you begin withdrawing the money. (Your company's human resources representative or your tax advisor can explain further.)

ARE MEDICAL BENEFITS COVERED?

What company benefits will end at your retirement? The most important is medical insurance. Will your company continue paying health insurance premiums for Medigap insurance (the part not covered by Medicare)? If you have company-paid life insurance or disability insurance, can you count on it in the future? Instead of funding retirees' future health insurance, many companies have chosen to reduce or eliminate it. Even if you start retirement with health insurance benefits, you may end up without it in the future.

Important! If you retire before age sixty-five (the age at which you become eligible for Medicare), will you have any health insurance? Buying it on the open market is very expensive.

Find out what the survivors' benefits of your pension are. Wives, unless you have a pension of your own, this will be very important to your future. But do not waive survivors' benefits unless you will have ample future income from other sources. Under law, a worker must have his spouse's written and notarized permission to remove her as a beneficiary of his pension.

If you are divorced, you are entitled to benefits under your spouse's pension if the marriage lasted ten years or longer and if you received them as part of your divorce settlement. If divorce should happen, consult an attorney for details about your pension rights.

The Employee Retirement Income Security Act of 1974 sets minimum standards for pension plans. For a more detailed explanation of ERISA and the various types of pension plans, see chapter 11 of *Social Security, Medicare and Pensions* by Joseph Matthews.

SAVINGS

After Social Security and pensions, whatever you have saved will have to work hard for you after retirement. This is the third leg of the stool.

People over sixty own a large percentage of our nation's assets. But assets are not income. That house is costing you money, not earning you anything, unless you can rent out part of it. What you need is cash to meet expenses, either now or in the future. How will you make your assets earn income? This will be the topic of the next chapter.

FEAR OF RETIREMENT

Many middle-aged Americans (ages forty-five to sixty-five) are afraid that they may not be able to retire in comfort. Observe the figures from a survey commissioned by the Merrill Lynch Company and reported in the May 1991 issue of *Money* Magazine:

- 23 percent of those over fifty-five said they are not ready financially for retirement, up seven points in one year.
- 93 percent voiced concern about health care costs, also up seven points in one year.
- 85 percent are afraid that nursing home costs could ruin them or their families financially.
- 90 percent think they will need financial help at some future time from their children or from the government, up from 79 percent the year before.
- 83 percent are afraid that their income will not meet their needs in the future, up from 74 percent in the previous year.

ESTIMATING YOUR LIVING COSTS

But take heart. Almost every retiree I've talked to has said, "I'm better off financially now that I'm retired than I was when I was working." Living expenses are lower. There are no longer any commuting costs or special clothing necessary for work. (My husband plans to hold a tie burning ceremony!) Couples may no longer need two cars. Your auto insurance costs will go down. You may own your home free and clear with no more monthly mortgage payments. And you'll find yourself eligible for all sorts of senior discounts.

On the down side, some expenses will go up. Medical and drug bills typically increase with age. Up to the present, medical costs have been growing much faster than inflation (18 percent over the past two years). The costs of medical insurance have been rising accordingly.

Even if your house is paid for, it will still need maintenance and repair, especially as it, too, gets older. Property taxes and utility bills usually increase. And of course, inflation—even a very low inflation rate of 4 or 5 percent per year—will drive all prices gradually upward.

Many retirement counselors use this rule of thumb: You will need 80 percent of your present income to maintain your current standard of living. The lower your present income, the higher the percentage you'll need in retirement. (Middle-income and upper-income people may need a much lower percentage because they no longer need to save and invest, and they have more room in their budgets to economize.)

Begin by adding up your present living expenses. Let's hope you have kept good records. If you need help in doing this, the money management books listed at the end of this chapter (which you may be able to get out of your public library) go into more detail.

Using bills, receipts, and canceled checks, reconstruct what you spend in an average year in each category: food, clothing, rent or mortgage payments, utilities, insurance, gifts or charitable donations, etc. Determine what percentage of your income is spent in each category.

This will help in your planning. When my husband and I did this, we found that mortgage payments that have been 25 percent of our pre-retirement income would be more than 50 percent of our retirement income. That just wouldn't work. It was clear that we would need to move to less expensive housing.

THE MOMENT OF TRUTH

Next, subtract whatever expenses you will no longer have after retirement. Add whatever new expenses you are likely to incur, such as Medigap insurance premiums. The figure you arrive at is the amount of income you will need in order to meet retirement living expenses.

Next, add up your income from Social Security, pension, interest on investments, etc. If this sum is not sufficient income, can you possibly reduce your expenses (by moving to less expensive housing, giving up one of your cars, etc.)?

Retirees are very creative about making do with less. We can all learn from our retired friends. Helen, for example, is always smartly dressed, yet spends very little on clothes. Her chic outfits come from a thrift store run by a local charity. The clothing is donated by wealthy women who wear it only once or twice.

Retirees can save money on food by forming a co-op with friends and neighbors and buying in quantity. Barter, both informal and formal, is an important fact of retirement life for many people. Usually, it's not called that. It's friends doing favors for each other. You cut my lawn, so I fix you a special meal or send over baked goods. I feed your pets while you're away, and you give me a ride when I need one.

Money can be saved on purchases by using cash instead of credit whenever possible. At 18 to 22 percent or more interest, credit cards are a drain on anyone's income, or as Proverbs 22:7 puts it, "The borrower is servant to the lender."

GOOD DEALS FOR SENIORS

Senior discounts are available on everything from checking accounts to travel. Restaurants, retail stores, service businesses, movie theaters, airlines, and hotels offer senior discounts to draw customers. A hospital in my community, John Muir Medical Center, through its "MuirCare 65" program, offers members over sixty-five waivers of hospital deductibles, co-insurance charges, and other out-of-pocket expenses, discounts on its emergency alert system, free health education seminars, personal assistance with insurance forms and medical paperwork, discounted nutrition counseling, a 20 percent discount in the hospital cafeteria, and free monthly blood pressure checkups.

Some of these discounts require a card, which is free for the asking, but many other merchants will give discounts if you ask for them. Businesses may not refer to them directly because some customers are offended when asked if they're eligible for a senior discount. It never hurts for you to ask.

In addition, low-income seniors are eligible for many special services that help them stay healthy and independent, such as Meals on Wheels, transportation to medical care, help with paying utility bills, etc. Those who don't qualify for free services can often get them for a reduced fee. For some, there is no income requirement. Contact your local Area Agency on Aging for details.

FRUGAL WITHOUT BEING A SCROOGE

A common problem in retirement, retirement counselors say, is to become obsessed with economizing. One or both marital partners will go to three different supermarkets to save ten cents on a can of beans. This can use up far too much time, and take all the joy out of your life. Be a smart shopper, but don't let the pursuit of savings take over your life.

Financial counselors see many clients who retire with substantial nest eggs yet don't feel secure. How much money is "enough"? For those who put all their faith and trust in money, there is never enough. Their problems are not financial, but spiritual. They are like the rich fool in Luke 12:13-21.

Some retirees never want to spend any of the nest egg they've accumulated. Financial counselors divide a person's life into five financial stages: protection, accumulation, conversion, preservation, and distribution. It's the last three that concern us at retirement, when we *convert* what we've saved into investments, try to *preserve* the purchasing power of our savings, and *distribute* our money either by spending it on our own needs or by giving it in our wills. Certainly by age seventy-five or so, it's safe to assume that the old age you've been saving for has arrived and it's okay to spend the money.

THE GREAT UNKNOWN: INFLATION

Inflation is a fact of life that keeps us running like mad just to stand still. Future rates of inflation are unknown, but retirement planners use the "rule of 72" as a rough indicator of what to expect. Divide 72 by the rate of inflation in order to find out how many years it will take for current prices to double. For example, if you divide 72 by 4 percent inflation, you are projecting that prices will double in eighteen years. Your present income will then buy only half as much.

Let's assume, as an example, that your retirement income is now $20,000 a year. At 4 percent inflation, in eighteen years you will need $40,000 a year to purchase the same things. At 7 percent inflation, it would take only ten years for prices to double. However, not all of your expenses will increase with inflation. If you own your home rather than renting, your housing costs will remain the same. Also, says financial expert Ron Blue, people who know how to manage money will consistently have a lower inflation rate than the national average.

HOW WILL YOU MEET INFLATION?

Where will the additional money you'll need come from? It could come from savings that you've invested. It could come from the equity in your house (inflation will increase its future value!). It could come from the cash value of life insurance policies. You may have to sell assets in order to meet living expenses.

If you have little or no money to invest at retirement, there is still something you can do. You might consider getting a part-time job so that you could save most of your earnings each month and allow that money to compound for a few years. You could then start withdrawing your interest and even principle as future prices rise.

MEDICAL COSTS—THE OTHER GREAT UNKNOWN

Retirees have always worried about inflation, but now the hot topic of conversation is medical costs and health insurance. Some retirees have seen their health insurance premiums rise 10 percent, 20 percent, or more in the past year alone because of skyrocketing medical costs.

Let's assume, for the sake of example, that medical costs and health insurance premiums continue to rise faster than inflation. At 10 percent per year, both would double in cost in seven years; at 20 percent, both would double in only three and a half years. Given a 20 percent increase annually, a health insurance policy costing $300 per month in 1991 would cost $600 in mid-1995. Medicine costing $100 per month in 1991 would cost $200 in mid-1995.

As a result of these kinds of increases, Medicare costs have tripled in the past ten years. The total for 1991 is expected to be $104 billion. Congress has reacted to the Medicare crisis by trying to rein in expenses while raising retirees' premiums and deductibles. You can probably expect your share of Medicare costs to rise in the future.

Medicare, by the way, is not free. You will be charged a premium and co-payments before Medicare begins to pay 80 percent, not 100 percent, of your medical costs. Hospitalization for even a few days could easily be $30,000 (or much more). Medicare pays 80 percent of that, or $24,000, leaving you responsible for $6,000. In order to protect themselves, most retirees buy additional policies, commonly known as Medigap policies, that pay the difference.

UNINSURED MEDICAL EXPENSES

It is important to remember that Medigap pays only for items Medicare covers. *If Medicare doesn't pay for it, Medigap doesn't either.* This leaves you responsible for, among other things, medicines, eyeglasses, hearing aids, dental work and dentures, and of course, home health care and nursing home care.

You are also responsible for doctors' fees above what Medicare allows. For example, if a doctor charges $5,000 for surgery and Medicare allows only $3,000, it will pay 80 percent of $3,000 (which is $2,400). Medigap insurance will pay your co-payment, which is 20 percent (in this case $600), and you will pay the remaining $2,000.

An important question to ask your present physician or any new physician you're considering is, "Do you take Medicare assignment?" This means, "Will you accept what Medicare allows as your fee in full?"

Joining a Health Maintenance Organization (HMO) is an option many retirees take to reduce their medical costs. But, since many HMOs have also been cutting services and some are financially shaky, be cautious, AARP warns.

Do you qualify for veterans' benefits? If so, some health care, perhaps even some long-term care, may be available to you. Contact your local VA office.

DON'T FALL FOR THE SCAMS

Many retirees buy unnecessary health insurance policies that they'll never collect on. Find a Medigap policy that meets your needs and, ignoring the ads, buy only what you need. Single disease coverage (for example, just for cancer) and coverage for hospitalization only, experts agree, are ordinarily a waste of money.

Until recently, thousands of Medigap policies offered a maze of confusing coverages. A Congressional investigation of Medigap abuses has led to a federal law, passed in 1990, which directs the National Association of Insurance Commissioners to design up to ten standard Medigap policies, each containing a core group of benefits. When these policies are ready (target date: the end of 1991), comparison shopping will be much easier. At that time, the selling of unapproved Medigap policies will become illegal.

For objective help in comparison shopping, many local senior centers, Area Agencies on Aging, and local AARP chapters have trained health insurance counselors. These volunteers can help you understand the policies you're considering.

WHAT ABOUT LONG-TERM CARE?

Neither Medicare nor Medigap policies cover long-term care (nursing homes). If your income is low, you can probably be covered in a nursing home under Medicaid. If you have $400,000 to $500,000 actively invested, you will probably be able to afford private nursing home services. It's the people in between who need to consider whether they should purchase long-term care insurance. Since the primary purpose of such insurance is to protect your assets if you should have to be in a nursing home, this is discussed in the next chapter under estate planning.

QUESTIONS FOR DISCUSSION

1. Draw up your estimates of retirement living and expenses.
2. Read and discuss some of the materials in the resource section for this chapter (page 232), either with other retirees or with your spouse (or both), in preparation for your more detailed financial planning for retirement.

CHAPTER EIGHTEEN

INVESTING FOR AN UNKNOWN FUTURE

There are two prevailing emotions when dealing with money: greed and fear.
A Financial Planner's Proverbial Saying

It's scary. There you are at retirement, either with your pension in a lump sum to invest or with your IRA or 401K nest egg, and the decisions you are about to make you'll have to both live *with* and live *on* for the rest of your life. Money lost through bad investments is not easily made up at our age. That's *fear.*

And waiting for us out there in the great, wide world of finance are all those people who can't wait to get their hands on our money. That's *greed.* Unless you're an experienced investor, it's a somewhat complex and risky place, this world of finances. And even then, you and I are no match for all the aggressive, money-hungry predators out there. We need help.

But before we seek investment and estate planning advice, we need to do our homework. Unless you master certain basics, you won't even know what questions to ask. You also need to try to remain humble. Read one or more of the recommended books on investing, and heed the warnings. You are not smarter than all those other people who have been burned. Try not to allow fear and greed to overwhelm you.

GETTING INFORMED AND KEEPING INFORMED

Be sure the advice you follow is current. Outdated knowledge is dangerous. We all just "knew" so many things that, we find out the hard way, are not necessarily the case—that real estate prices will always rise, that there is no risk to buying government-insured CDs,[1] that banks and insurance companies are always "safe."

There's strength in numbers. Why not get together with other retirees—friends or fellow church members—and form a club to study investments? Perhaps you can find some local retiree who is an experienced investor to help answer your questions. Or you could read one of the recommended books together with a group and discuss it.

One group that did just that even produced their own book. It's *Finances After 50: Financial Planning for the Rest of Your Life* by Dorlene V. Shane and the United Seniors Health Cooperative. You may be able to find it, as I did, in your public library. It includes worksheets that help you figure out your net worth, plan a budget, understand various investment options, etc.

IT'S ALL YOURS—OR IS IT?

You can't get out of the responsibility of being a good steward of your finances. And if you believe, as I do, that the money is not really yours but *God's*, the obligation to take care of it is a sacred one. You can't just automatically turn it over to somebody else to manage for you.[2] That person may just manage it out of existence.

Author and investment broker Gary D. Moore quotes a proverbial saying among brokers: "Financial counselors start with experience and their clients start with money. When they end up, the counselors have the money and the clients have the experience."

Women of my generation are especially prone to think men are "supposed" to know all about investments the way they're "supposed" to know all about automobiles. But more than one man has confessed to me that he knows nothing about modern engines. When something goes wrong, those men just throw open the hood and try to look wise.

You can't assume that the husband, just because he's male, is qualified by virtue of his gender to make all the financial decisions for both of you. Statistically, the chances are that most women will become widows. At widowhood, the husband's pension is usually cut in two, and the widow is going to be dependent on investment income for support. Her future security depends on the decisions that are made now.

"I always recommend that a husband train his wife . . . to manage whatever God has entrusted to them. Otherwise, she has been effectively disinherited," says Ron Blue.[3]

A FEW BASICS FOR STARTERS

This brief chapter can't even begin to scratch the surface of the world of finance. But it can provide a few principles that, if you hold on to them firmly, will help you understand what you're doing. If you're expecting new and revolutionary ideas, you're going to be disappointed. Investments change, but principles don't. These principles are ancient wisdom, much of which can be found in the Bible, and they are as true today as they ever were.

UNDERSTANDING INVESTMENTS

You need to invest, not speculate. Many people don't understand the difference. An investment has a great probability to earn you money, and you can reasonably expect to sell it for more than you paid for it. A speculation is a gamble that something is going up in price in the future. If you must gamble, do it with your friends over a game of *Monopoly*, where you're dealing with play money. Don't use your retirement savings.

Buying quality stocks to hold for years is an investment. Buying stocks based on a "hot tip," and then trading them when the market rises and falls is speculation. Real estate earning income that exceeds expenses is an investment. Gold, diamonds, jewelry, art, baseball cards, oil leases, commodities futures, junk bonds, and penny stocks are speculations. The people who sell you these things will have their commissions even if prices go down; you could end up with nothing.[4]

Investments represent either loans or ownership. When you buy bonds, you're lending money, and that money earns you interest. But when you buy real estate or stock, you become an owner. You make money when you sell whatever you own—*if* it has increased in value.

In the past, retirees were advised to invest for income, so many people converted all their assets into loan types of investments that produced interest income—such as certificates of deposit, municipal bonds, treasury bonds, etc. However, investment counselors warn, this is a very dangerous strategy for someone who is going to live for twenty or more years.

Loan types of investments do not keep pace with inflation, and they run the risk of falling interest rates, which can drastically reduce your income. For income protection you need some of your nest egg in ownership types of investments, such as real estate and stocks.

UNDERSTANDING RISKS

There are no investments without risk. There are only degrees of risk. Often risks are overlooked. Chapters 21 to 28 in Jane Bryant Quinn's book do an excellent job of listing the various risks of each type of investment.

Risk rises with return. You can absolutely depend on this correlation. If anyone tries to sell you an investment that pays a high rate of return and this person tells you it's low-risk, he or she is either lying or doesn't understand the investment. Beware: Many investments look good only because the risks are well-concealed. A safe, steady rise over time will beat "get rich quick" investments every time.[5]

An investment that is a high risk during times of high inflation may be a low risk during a recession, and vice versa. As a general rule, when stock prices rise, interest rates fall, and vice versa. Therefore, there is no one best investment for all phases of the economic cycle. Wise investors take this into account by *diversifying* their investments. It's the old "don't put all your eggs in one basket" axiom. If one type of investment is down, there is a likelihood that some of the others will be up.[6]

The* promised *return and the* actual *return are not always the same. The "actual return" is what you get after allowing for inflation, taxes, commissions, and management fees. It's very easy for clever marketing people to make the numbers look better than they really are.[7]

You may be your own worst enemy. People's fear leads them to buy and sell at the worst possible times. Their greed leads them to look only at the promised rate of return and not at the risks. And their fear causes them to panic and sell when, in fact, it is the most opportune time to buy.

SHOULD YOU PAY CASH FOR A HOUSE?

Many retirees who move want to pay cash for their new homes without taking out a mortgage. Some people need the security of owning a home free and clear. *But* paying cash may not always be the wisest thing to do.

On the pro side, during times of low interest rates, paying off the mortgage may be the best return you can get. If your present mortgage interest is 10 percent and you pay it off, that's like earning 10 percent on your money. Consider this: If you don't pay it off, is there any other investment that would earn you 10 percent on your money? But real estate is not *liquid*—that is, it can't be converted into cash easily.

However, if you have a large equity built up in your home and need cash later, you don't necessarily have to sell the house. You can convert your equity into monthly cash payments by using a "Home Equity Conversion" (also called a reverse mortgage). No repayment is due until you die or move. The house is then sold and the mortgage lender is repaid. See the free AARP publication entitled *Home-Made Money: Consumer's Guide to Home Equity Conversion* for more information.

Here are some disadvantages of paying all cash for your house, as listed by Robert J. Bruss, a real estate attorney and writer of a nationally syndicated real estate column:

- You lose the use of funds you could have invested elsewhere.
- You lose the interest deduction on your income tax.
- You sell securities in order to pay cash, thus having to pay a tax on the profits.
- You later need to take out a home equity loan, you can deduct interest up to only $100,000.
- One of you needs to enter a nursing home, you will not be able to shelter any assets in your home.
- You lose the inflation hedge of paying off the mortgage in cheaper dollars.

Only an accountant or financial planner who knows your individual situation can help you make this decision to pay off your home.

SEEKING WISE COUNSEL

Proverbs 14:15 says that a naive person believes everything, but a prudent person considers all his steps. Only very naive persons would take investment advice from a stranger who calls them on the phone, or from unknown "financial experts" who give seminars about some new "investment opportunity" at hotels and motels.

If you get one of these calls, say courteously, "I never respond to telephone solicitors. Thank you. Goodbye." And hang up.

These telephone callers are invariably salespeople who are interested in earning commissions, not in preserving and increasing your nest egg. Also, many who call themselves "investment counselors" and "financial counselors" are really brokers, in other words salesmen who make their living by earning commissions whenever someone buys or sells.

Only the very naive would expect a salesperson whose ethics they know nothing about *not* to recommend the investments that pay them the highest commissions (some as high as 50 percent). As a general rule, the riskier the investments, the higher the commissions. How else would the companies that put these deals together unload them?

Where, then, are you going to find an investment advisor you can trust? Are there such persons? Yes, but you have to find them; you can't wait for them to come to you.

ASK FOR RECOMMENDATIONS

Financial planners earn their living in two basic ways: either from commissions on what they sell you, or from fees. But you can't conclude that financial planners who earn commissions are less ethical than those who charge fees. There are unethical and/or incompetent people in both groups. It's just that fee-only planners have less incentive to manipulate the truth.

However, not everybody can afford the fees of fee-only planners, so many legitimate planners charge a combination of a low fee plus a commission. So, how can you know if someone is competent? It's not always easy because financial planners are not licensed or regulated in any way by the state or federal government. Anyone can call himself or herself a financial planner. If a planner represents only one company, he or she may in reality be a salesperson or broker, and not a planner at all.

Choose a financial planner as carefully as you would a physician or an attorney. Word-of-mouth recommendations from your friends, your accountant or attorney, bank officer, or other retirees would be a good way to begin. Two organizations that certify planners, thus showing they have had specialized training, can provide the names of their graduates in your area. Write to the International Association for Financial Planning, 2 Concourse Parkway, Suite 800, Atlanta, GA 30328, or Institute of Certified Financial Planners, 3443 South Galena, Suite 190, Denver, CO 80231-5093.

If the planner you are considering is not certified by one of these organizations, is he or she credentialed by other organizations? For example, those who give stock market investment advice must be licensed by the Securities and Exchange Commission. If this person is an accountant, is he or she a CPA? If a lawyer, a member of the Bar Association? A person who sells insurance company products may be a CLU (Certified Life Underwriter).

In order to receive recognition from these organizations, all these people must have passed tests requiring a high level of competency. You can check on whether any complaints have been registered against this person by contacting the credentials organization or your local Better Business Bureau.

You want someone who is not a beginner. He or she should have been in practice through at least one business cycle. For a list of helpful questions to ask when hiring financial planners, see *Money Matters: How to Talk to and Select Lawyers, Financial Planners, Tax Preparers and Real Estate Brokers* (published by AARP in cooperation with the Federal Trade Commission).

Keep in mind that no financial plan is suitable forever. Conditions change and financial plans must be reviewed periodically. Will your planner help you do that?

It's vitally important that you remember not to give a financial planner a blank check to wheel and deal with your money. In fact, before signing up with anyone, I'd recommend reading chapter 23, "Working with a Stockbroker," in Jane Bryant Quinn's book, *Making the Most of Your Money*. Many of the same warnings about stockbrokers also apply to financial planners. She gives you some tips on protecting yourself. For insight into why the modern, deregulated "financial supermarket" is such a mine field for investors, read chapter 10, "Choosing Investment Counsel," in Gary D. Moore's book, *The Thoughtful Christian's Guide to Investing*.

Before you talk to a planner, you will need to figure out your net worth so that you know how much you have to work with. Your net worth is the sum you get when you add up all your assets (equity in your house, cars, bank accounts, stocks, bonds, CDs, IRAs, 401Ks) and then subtract your liabilities (money owed on loans, etc.). Most of the recommended books give more detailed instructions for doing this.

TAKING THE MONEY OUT

Keep very good records. You need to have in your file of important papers (where you keep such documents as copies of your will, instructions to your heirs, locations of your bank accounts and safe deposit boxes, the names of your attorneys and financial advisors, etc.) a complete list of your investments, showing the date acquired, how much your paid for them, and all statements received.

Six months after you turn seventy, you are required by law to begin withdrawing money from your IRAs. And the taxes on those investments, which you have deferred for all those years, now become due. You will need an accountant's advice on how to take out this money without paying unnecessary taxes, and for that you will have to know how much you originally paid, which part was principle and which interest, etc. Believe me, it can get complicated enough even if you have complete records. Without them, it will be total chaos.

SENIORS TARGETED AS FRAUD VICTIMS

American consumers lose $1 billion per year to telephone swindlers. An additional $1.8 billion is lost to mail order frauds. Many of the victims are seniors, because not only do many seniors have money, but they're often vulnerable to high-pressure tactics. I am less worried about my ability to cope with con artists now than sometime down the road when I may be less mentally alert, or lonely and emotionally vulnerable.[8]

Widows routinely can expect to get calls from con artists soon after the husband's death. (The vultures who prey on widows read the obituaries, you may be sure.) At this highly emotional time, it may be hard for you to resist the friendly, ingratiating voice at the other end of the line. But do so. Hang up immediately.

Cults are increasingly targeting the elderly, according to the

Cult Awareness Network of Chicago. There are religious groups, political groups, and other sweet-talking gold diggers who will use guilt and intimidation tactics to tap into the wealth of older people in order to fill the pockets of the cultic entrepreneurs.[9]

BANK AND INSURANCE COMPANY FAILURES

The greed, mismanagement, recklessness, deceit, and fraudulent conduct of businesses that most people once considered trustworthy boggles the mind. In the past five years there have been 896 bank failures (compared to 840 for the previous fifty years), which has depleted the FDIC Bank Insurance Fund to the brink of insolvency. Taxpayers will be paying billions over the next few years to clean up this mess.

Many banks, S & L's, and other institutions still sell uninsured CDs. Your only protection is to be certain your money is *federally* (not state) insured and that you keep no more than $100,000 in any one account. The state takeover of Executive Life Insurance Company, leaving thousands of retirees' savings and pensions in jeopardy, has sent a shock wave of fear through the financial community about the general safety of insurance companies. If you invest in insurance products, such as annuities, choose only the top-rated companies.

MISTAKES DO HAPPEN

Despite your best efforts to be cautious, mistakes in financial management do happen. Sometimes, a professional will give you what he thinks is the best advice at the time, and because of conditions beyond his control, he can be wrong. You may think you know what you're doing and find out later that you didn't really understand an investment, or that you were deceived. Everybody may act impulsively or emotionally at times and make mistakes.

If it happens to you, you can do one of two things. You can say "I learned a lesson the hard way. This was unfortunate, but I need to get on with the business of living," *or* you can let the experience ruin your life. If you've been cheated, you will understandably be angry. If you've made what you believe was a "dumb" mistake, you'll be angry at yourself, and even need to forgive yourself.

WHY ESTATE PLANNING?

I never thought of myself as having an estate, but when you think about it, everybody has some assets. Of course, you have a will, right? If you don't, the state law will decide how your assets will be distributed, and you may not like the results—if you were around to observe the whole procedure.

Many couples try to get around the need for a will by holding all property jointly. However, depending on state law, how assets are held has important consequences as far as taxes and qualifying for Medicaid are concerned. Also, suppose you both die together in an auto accident? One of you will die intestate.

If you want money to pass directly to a child at your death, instead of giving him joint tenancy on your account (which has many disadvantages), you can set up a signature account with him as beneficiary. See your bank for details.

If your estate will be a small one, a simple will that you fill out yourself and have notarized is perfectly legal. If you do it right, it's fine. But I would not be comfortable with it. If your estate is at all sizable, you definitely need advice from an attorney who is an expert at estate planning and/or elder law. Couples in second marriages who wish to separate their money and leave their estates to their own children or grandchildren will also have more complicated wills. You will need expert legal advice.

DO YOU NEED A TRUST?

In addition to drawing up a will, you may want your attorney to draw up a *revocable trust*, also known as a *living trust*. By putting your assets in a trust, with yourself as trustee, you continue to have full use and control. However, at your death, instead of going through probate, your assets pass directly to the other trustee, usually a spouse. This can save a great deal of money on taxes and probate costs, depending on the laws of your state. An estate planning attorney can explain further and help you decide whether this is the best thing for you to do.

In some states, attorneys are aggressively marketing living trusts, but there are disadvantages. Setting up a trust can be costly and cumbersome, and it can make a beneficiary ineligible for SSI and Medicaid. Trusts set up by married couples usually require both signatures before changes can be made. If one marital partner becomes mentally incompetent, the spouse might end up in a lot of difficulty.

Attorneys specializing in estate planning, like other professionals, can be found through word-of-mouth recommendations or recommendations of a financial planner, a trusted accountant, or your local Area Agency on Aging. If you can't afford an attorney, your local AAA can also steer you to sources of free or low-cost legal advice.

Even if you decide against a revocable trust, documents that everybody ought to have include *a living will, a durable power of attorney,* and *a durable power of attorney for health care* (in states where the latter is allowed). A living will states your wishes if you should become incapacitated. A durable power of attorney gives someone you trust the legal power to act in your behalf, and goes into effect only if you become incapacitated. Durable power of attorney for health care gives the person you name the right to make health decisions for you if you are not able to make them for yourself at some future time. Married couples usually name each other to act for them. Single and newly widowed people need to choose a trusted relative or friend who will see that their wishes are honored.

Many retirees also purchase burial plots at this time. Some arrange to prepay funeral expenses. Others set aside funds for these expenses.

PRUDENT GIVING

If you plan to give money in your will to your church or favorite charity, there may be ways that you can have your cake and eat it, too. Property, such as all or even part of a house, for example, can be given to a charity during your lifetime, enabling you to take a tax deduction for the gift in the year that you give it. But you still have the right to live in it for the rest of your life (that's called "life interest"). It passes to the charity after your death without becoming part of your estate.

Another vehicle for charitable giving is a pooled income fund. This is a trust formed to pay anyone you name, such as your favorite charity, as a beneficiary. You receive the earnings for life, get a tax deduction, and the principle goes to the charity after you die.

If your estate is sizable, you may want to have your own attorney set up a trust. But every religious denomination and charity has people on staff who can give you information or guide you in setting up a way of donating that will be most advantageous for you. Ask about help with estate planning; they'll be happy to assist.

WHAT ABOUT GIFTS?

Should you give money or property to your children while you're still living? Only you can decide that, but there are some important considerations.

How will it affect your relationship with your children? Do they need the money, or are you making life too easy for them, or trying to win them or control them? Will the gift affect your ability to take care of yourself in the future?

What are the tax consequences? Never make a sizable gift without consulting your tax advisor. If you give too much, you will pay a federal gift tax. If the gift is a house, your child may some day have to pay a huge tax on the profits that he would not have had to pay if he had inherited it.

If the child is married, how stable is the marriage? If this child should divorce, your gifts could become part of the community property or divorce settlement.

PROVIDING FOR LONG-TERM CARE

At $30,000 per year, how many years would it take for you to use up all your assets for nursing home care? For most people, the answer is *not very long*. Because people are living longer, it has become necessary to take not only death but also late-life illness and frailty into account when you plan for the future. The time to think about nursing home protection is when you do your pre-retirement financial and estate planning.

Only people with over $400,000 actively invested can expect to generate enough income to pay nursing home costs. That takes care of the rich. Some states have maximum income requirements for Medicaid set so low that only the very poorest can qualify. This leaves a vast number of people in the middle unprotected. Unless the present laws change, what can they do?

One possible way to raise the money for long-term care are Accelerated Death Benefits insurance policies. Accelerated Death Benefits are available as a rider on a life insurance policy. Some companies will add it to existing policies for an additional premium. Instead of paying the beneficiary after your death, ADBs begin paying while you are alive if certain conditions are met, such as terminal illness, "dread disease," or nursing home placement. This plan needs to be compared with borrowing against the cash value of the policy. You could also raise the money by borrowing against the cash value of the policy—then you'd have to pay interest. This may be less costly than an ADB. You'll need to compare costs.

IS NURSING HOME INSURANCE THE ANSWER?

Most major insurance companies now offer long-term care insurance policies, which usually pay a certain number of dollars per day for stays of one to three years in an intermediate or skilled nursing facility. Some also pay for at-home health care. How much you will pay for the policy depends on how old you are when you enroll and the specified benefits. It will not be cheap.

If you decide that long-term care insurance should be part of your estate planning, proceed with caution. State insurance commissioners and consumer groups have found, after ten years' experience with this type of insurance, that over 60 percent of the people who bought it and later entered a nursing facility never collected a cent. Even when benefits were paid, they were usually far below actual nursing home costs and lapsed before the nursing home stay ended.

As a result, rules have been tightened in many states. Few policies now limit nursing home care payment to patients who have been hospitalized first. Most no longer exclude Alzheimer's patients. But it's important to examine and compare the policies very carefully, not just the brochures.

Fifteen years or more down the road, when you may need the coverage, a lot of unfortunate things could happen:

- Premiums may go up so much that you can no longer afford them, and thus drop the policy.
- Nursing home costs may go up so much that the per diem coverage allowed will be grossly inadequate. Look for a policy with an inflation adjustment clause.
- Perhaps there are so many conditions and exclusions that you will never be able to collect on the policy. Read the conditions and exclusions part of the policy very carefully.

■ The company may go bankrupt or be taken over by another company. Buy only from a company top-ranked by A.M. Best (which you can look up in the library), and look for a policy that cannot be canceled by the company (a policy that has a guaranteed renewal). Such a policy cannot raise the premiums except as spelled out in the original policy. (Increases to keep pace with inflation are reasonable.)

PROTECTING THE AT-HOME SPOUSE

What if one spouse should have to enter a nursing home? The costs could take all the nest egg and leave the at-home spouse destitute, without a nest. Formerly, if the wife went into a nursing home, the husband got to keep the assets that were in his name. This is no longer the case. Transferring assets to a spouse, which used to be a strategy for protecting the at-home spouse, no longer works.

There are ways of protecting the at-home spouse, but the rules are so bizarre that you probably need an attorney's guidance to do it. Many attorneys who specialize in estate planning also practice what they call elder law, which is primarily Medicaid planning. You can find such a specialist through their professional association, the National Academy of Elder Law Attorneys.

First, let me review the current Medicaid rules. After all the patient's money is gone, he or she can go on Medicaid, which is state-administered. Medicaid rules require that you "spend down" your assets to $2,000 before you can qualify. The patient's home is exempt if the spouse of the nursing home patient or some other family caregiver is living in it. Certain other assets are also exempt. Rules vary by state.

If the patient is married, the couple's assets are divided. The at-home spouse gets to keep either half of the combined assets or $62,580, whichever is greater. Once a husband goes into a nursing home, the wife loses his entire pension income, which, by law, must go for his care (except for a $900 per month basic living allowance). She'll have to dip into the remaining assets (that amount cannot exceed $62,580) that she's allowed to keep in order to pay her living expenses. But before long, that will be gone. After her husband's death, she'll be left with her Social Security pension to live on. If she's fortunate, they might have owned a house, which she gets to keep. She can sell that and invest the proceeds, or try to get a Reverse Annuity Mortgage.

But will that be enough?

One protection for the spouse might be putting assets into an *irrevocable trust*. The assets can't be touched, so they don't count toward a Medicaid "spend down," but the owner loses control over them. He can spend the income but not the principle, which goes to his heirs. If he's in a nursing home, after his death his wife would inherit the proceeds of the trust.

Can you give away assets to your children before you enter a nursing home? No, unless you do it at least thirty months before. But you can put money into your house, which is protected. (This is where renting or owning your home free and clear is a disadvantage.)

Is this legal? Yes. Is it ethical? Some groups think not.

John Milgate, an attorney who specializes in elder law, does not question how ethical it may be. What's *really* unethical, he says, is a system so complicated that people have to go to an attorney or end up being badly hurt because they didn't understand the law.

"Hiding assets is illegal and I won't do it," Milgate says. "But an irrevocable trust is not hiding assets; it's permissible under the law. If a rule is known to lawmakers, it's not a loophole. A loophole is something that the law did not intend."

Of course, by the time you read this, the rules may have changed—again. Be sure to check with your local Area Agency on Aging or an attorney specializing in elder law for an update.

THE LAST STEP

After you've put your financial house in order, sit back and relax. Make sure you organize your important papers, storing the originals in a safe-deposit box and keeping copies in your file of important documents, which you will review and update yearly.

QUESTIONS FOR DISCUSSION

1. Continue with the recommended reading from the previous chapter.
2. Organize your files.
3. Figure out your net worth.

PART FIVE

WHEN THE SPIRIT IS WILLING BUT THE BODY IS WEAK

CHAPTER NINETEEN

ATTITUDE IS EVERYTHING

Few people know how to be old.
LaRochefoucauld

How do you learn how to be old? You look around for models. The kind of old people I like to be around are those who accept themselves without apology just the way they are, and even manage a sense of humor about what's happening to them. Kathleen Fischer tells of coming upon a couple in a senior center who were laughing over an anonymous poem that they were reading together:

> "Everything is farther away than it used to be.
> It's twice as far to the corner and they've added a hill, I've noticed.
> I've given up running for the bus.
> It leaves faster than it used to."

In one sense, she comments, this is a description of the slowing down that comes with age. This could lead to feelings of hopelessness. But humor puts it in a different perspective, transforming difficulties and even indignities into laughter.

> Humor recognizes the tragedy of the human condition. . . . But by laughing at this condition, we declare that it is not final. It can be overcome. Humor is a gentle reminder of

> the reality of redemption. Redemptive humor is more than the ability to enjoy an isolated humorous situation. It's an attitude toward all of life.[1]

LAUGHTER—THE BEST MEDICINE

Humor is also a choice. When someone made a remark to Doug that he thought was infuriating, he told himself, "I can either get mad, or I can laugh." He decided to laugh, and telling about it later, he was able to share his laughter.

With humor we transcend our limitations. There's an anonymous verse written by an aging person that concludes with the line, "My get up and go has got up and went." Those who are wise wave goodbye to their "get up and go" not only with a tear but also with a chuckle.

Those who choose humor have made what Robert C. Peck calls a vital choice in the later years: "ego transcendence over ego preoccupation." They are able to say, in effect, "Yes, my bodily strength is declining and I know I'm getting closer to death, but my self (the ego) is much more than this puny, insignificant body. My continued existence on this earth is not the most important thing in the world, after all." As a sociologist, Peck uses secular rather than religious terms. I would call it "having our minds on God rather than having our minds on ourselves."

People with this attitude compensate for a decline in strength of the body. They have learned how to cope.

All our lives we've been using either successful or unsuccessful coping strategies to handle the normal stresses and strains of life. Unsuccessful strategies include smoking, numbing our feelings with drugs and alcohol, overeating, excessive TV watching, blowing our stacks, suppressing our feelings, etc. These seem to work in the short run, but in the long run, they're destructive. Toward the end of life, they catch up with us with a vengeance.

ACCENTUATE THE POSITIVE

Successful coping strategies (in addition to humor) include prayer and meditation, physical exercise, talking things out with a friend or confidant, and developing the habit of praise (overcoming negativity).

Probably the greatest attitude problem as we age is negativity. The "naysayer" in your head will always be pointing out what you can't do and what you're missing, if you let him. It takes practice to focus on what we *can do* and what we still have going for us. Research has shown that older people with a positive mental outlook rate their own health as much better than it "really" is by any objective standard.[2]

Learning how to handle our emotions is increasingly important as we age if we're to avoid getting mired in depression. With age comes loss, and with loss comes grief. One of the leading causes of depression in older people is unresolved grief. Grief can be worked through and depressions do lift, but you have to believe that you can be helped.

Some strategies to build *inner strength* are discussed in chapter 21.

CARE, NOT CURE

Taking care of our health will slow but cannot stop the aging process. As the years go by we are changing, often in ways over which we have little control. We can learn to care for our bodies as we age, but we can't "cure" old age. It's not a disease.

But we can take heart for our own situation. Many of the negative changes that we see in older people are *not* the result of normal aging, but of disease. A "healthy old age" is not a contradiction in terms.

How well we adapt to the normal changes of aging bodies is largely a function of how well we're willing to face reality. For example, older people don't see or hear as well as they once did. They often need brighter lights in their homes and stronger eyeglasses. They may need amplifiers on their telephone receivers, or they may need to wear hearing aids in order to hear well enough to communicate with others.

If, when these changes come upon us, we take steps to adapt, we can continue to function normally. But if we try to pretend we can get along without hearing aids or stronger glasses, denying that we need these helps because that would mean admitting we're "old," we cut ourselves off from life. Isolation from people will then really send us into a decline!

SHORT-TERM MEMORY PROBLEMS

Often, when aging people forget a name or a date, they panic, certain that senile dementia is just around the corner. But everybody forgets sometimes. When this happens to a younger person, we think nothing of it.

I like the style of Harold "Doc" Edgerton, an M.I.T. professor emeritus, inventor of Sonar and the strobe light for electronic flash photography, and holder of forty-seven patents. At the age of eighty-five, he was giving his annual lecture at M.I.T. when he suddenly drew a blank and began stammering. There was an embarrassed silence as he realized he could not remember something he "should" have known.

Finally, he said, "Well, I used to know that. In fact, I wrote a book about it, and I'm old enough to have a right to forget it. So look in the book." The audience burst into applause.

This story gives us all permission to have a less than perfect memory. If someone as distinguished as Professor Edgerton can forget something, so can I.

MENTAL ABILITY IN OLD AGE

Do you fear losing your mind as you age? The percentage of people with Alzheimer's and other dementias is small, although it rises with advanced age. Many so-called "senile" older people are really suffering from some treatable disorder, such as poor nutrition or over-medication.

In one study of healthy males by Robert N. Butler, M.D., intellectual performance of older adults was superior to the young control group. But the healthiest older sample did better on the tests than a group in poorer health, "suggesting the sensitivity of cognition to health."[3]

Indeed, mental changes in older adults frequently have some physical cause that ought to be investigated. Vernon Mark, M.D., a neurosurgeon and medical researcher, lists ten treatable causes of memory loss in older patients: clinical depression, fluid imbalance, drug overdose, malnutrition, too much insulin (in diabetics), anemia and lung disease, head injury, small strokes, poor blood circulation (which can be caused by too much blood pressure medication, which lowers the blood pressure too much and can contribute to other circulatory problems), and severe hypothyroidism. When these conditions are treated, the memory loss and other mental problems often go away.

It used to be thought that intelligence peaked in early adulthood, but further investigation has proved that this just isn't so.

"Intelligence" is actually a cluster of abilities. There is a decline with age in the ability to acquire new information, but no decline in the ability to process the accumulated wisdom and knowledge of a lifetime. This does not mean that older people can't learn new information; it means that they learn it more slowly than they once did.[4] This has been proven by people who've gone to college in their sixties and seventies and competed successfully with twenty-year-olds.

PLAY TO YOUR STRENGTHS

What's that saying on coffee mugs? "Age and cunning will win out every time over youth and talent." The old excel at problem solving.

People who stay mentally alert as they age have learned to play to this advantage in acquired wisdom, and to their other strengths. Athletes adapt; a tennis player who can no longer run very fast learns, if he keeps on playing the game, to place the ball so that his opponent has to do most of the running. Similarly, people can adapt mentally.

For example, you can learn to depend less on your memory and more on written notes and reminders. Memory training courses (which you will find at some senior centers and universities) teach strategies for making the memory more efficient. One simple trick is simply to pay closer attention to what you're doing. Instead of parking your car and sticking your keys in your pocket, take time to notice the row and number you're in, writing it down if necessary, and to notice which door of the building you enter.

Visualization is another useful trick. One ancient mnemonic (memory) device is, when going through a well-known building or street, to mentally store some new facts you have learned within the rooms of the building or about the houses on this street. Then, later, you can mentally walk through the building, visualizing what's there, and you can recall those new facts in each place along the way.

USE IT OR LOSE IT

Memory researchers have found that anything associated with an unusual event will be remembered because the brain releases a chemical that "fixes" it in the mind. That's the danger, after retirement, of leading an eventless life. Everything fades into the same dull background and nothing stands out as memorable.

The most important help for the aging brain is mental stimulation—the old "use it or lose it" principle. Brains, like muscles, need exercise in order to function. Doing what you enjoy, being with people, using your accumulated experience, keeping up with what's going on in the world, perhaps taking part in a volunteer activity—all these things can keep you mentally healthy. Doing nothing, or merely "filling time" with activities that are meaningless and unrewarding, can lead to both mental and physical decline.

QUESTIONS FOR DISCUSSION

1. Maggie Kuhn, founder of the Gray Panthers, advises, "Do one new thing every week; learn one new thing every day." What new things are you doing or learning?
2. Are you using any of the negative coping strategies mentioned earlier (smoking, numbing your feelings with drugs and alcohol, overeating, excessive TV-watching, blowing your stack, suppressing your feelings)? How can you change?
3. Which of the positive coping strategies should you be working on?

CHAPTER TWENTY

AN OUNCE OF PREVENTION

Eat, drink and be leary.
O. Henry

L*eary* is an old-fashioned word, little used nowadays. To "be leary" means to beware, to watch out for the consequences of something. As we age, we need to beware of eating and drinking *too much*, especially of the wrong things. The punishment for overindulgence is not an early death, but something far worse.

What could be worse?

As the author of *Age Wave* said, "I observed that a lifetime of disregard for personal health usually led . . . to chronic disease, *a kind of extended life imprisonment*. It was obvious that many of the painful, punishing *illnesses of old age could have been prevented*."[1]

Heart attacks, strokes, cancer, diabetes, emphysema, depression—all preventable? Well, these are all largely *lifestyle* diseases, aggravated and intensified not by the aging process but by the way we live. The evidence is very strong, but convincing people that they ought to change the way they're living is a hard sell.

When I mentioned "healthy lifestyles" to my husband, he said, "I'm not interested in healthy lifestyles, whatever that is. All I care about is being able to continue doing what I enjoy doing."

"Same thing!" I said.

WE "LEARN" TO BE SICK OLD PEOPLE

Take the risk factors in cardiovascular disease (heart attacks, strokes, etc.): Smoking, use of drugs, unhealthy diets, no exercise, and poor stress management are all socially learned behavior. People growing up in the United States *learn* how to age in poor health. Our culture teaches it.

In the 1970s, anthropologists working in the Abkhasian region of the Caucasus Mountains of the Soviet Union reported on a group of rural villagers living in good health to fabulous ages—120 to 150 years. We now know that these claims were exaggerated; the hardy villagers were actually about 90 to 100 years old. But they were still extraordinary old people, and their vigor was largely due to their healthy lifestyle.

> Abkhasian *cultural* conceptions of proper diet, age-based behaviors, and other activities promoting long life share a number of common factors with the behavior of healthy centenarians in the United States and other countries. Such persons tend to have low-fat, low-calorie diets; refrain from much caffeine, tobacco and alcohol; have been physically active throughout their lives and are well integrated into their communities.[2]

HOW DID WE GET THIS WAY?

Americans did not always live the way we do now. If you grew up when I did, during the Great Depression and World War II, your parents probably were not able to afford rich food. A chicken or a roast was for Sunday, not for every single day. Cake or pie for dessert was also reserved for Sunday, or for company meals. I drank milk or water—soda pop was for special occasions. I saved my pennies to buy candy *occasionally* at the corner candy store. *Occasionally* my parents took me to the ice cream parlor to get cones as a treat.

We walked about a mile in each direction to get there. In fact, to get anywhere, we walked or took a bus because most people did not own cars. (Or if they did, during World War II, wartime gasoline rationing restricted their use.) Meat, sugar, butter, and many other foods were also rationed during the war. There were fewer labor-saving machines at home or at work. Both men and women worked much harder physically.

Although it may sound as if we were deprived, obesity, a major health risk factor, rarely occurred before middle age. Young men were leaner. I don't remember any men in their twenties with potbellies. The word *stress* was not in people's everyday vocabulary or in their thoughts. People suffered from "nerves," but they managed to handle their anxieties without recourse to mind-altering drugs or psychologists. The pace of life was slower and families were more stable. Life was by no means utopian, but it seemed a lot more manageable.

Do you remember it this way, too?

So, when did everything change?

After World War II, the United States said farewell to a life of poverty and self-denial and hello to affluence! Incomes went up, and consumer goods proliferated as wartime restrictions were lifted.

Supermarkets sprang up, filled with a cornucopia of foods. People could and did eat meat every day, in prodigious quantities. If you wanted ice cream, you could buy it by the half-gallon in the supermarket, take it home to your freezer, and consume it every day if you wanted to. Almost overnight, vending machines with candy bars and soft drinks were everywhere. New snack foods were invented. Fast food restaurants with high-fat menus became part of our lives.

Now people could afford to buy automobiles and drive everywhere. Machinery replaced human labor at home and in the shop. Everybody got TV sets, and formed the habit of snacking while watching television. We became a nation of watchers of sporting events—from the fifties to the seventies (when jogging was first popularized), people who exercised were considered eccentric.

Is it any wonder that obesity is a national health menace? Heart disease has become epidemic. It's now the leading cause of death in *both* women and men.

WE *CAN* DO SOMETHING

"Coronary heart disease is largely a disease of excess," says Dean Ornish, M.D., a researcher who has proved scientifically that removing excess fat from the diet and excess stress from one's life can *reverse the physical changes* in diseased arteries, which lead to heart attacks and strokes.[3] Heart disease and the other "lifestyle diseases" are diseases caused by affluence. We're eating ourselves not only to death, but also to chronic diseases that make old age miserable.

John W. Rowe, M.D., president of the Mount Sinai School of Medicine in New York, distinguishes between "usual aging" and "successful aging." If you remove individuals with disease from the group of aging people under study, he says, "the effects of age on a number of important variables, especially in the cardiovascular system, are minimal. . . . There may be less to aging than we thought."[4]

If you want to reduce the risk of spending the final years of your life in a wheelchair or in a nursing home, unable to get out of bed unaided, here is what you need to do:

1. *If you smoke, stop.*
2. *Exercise daily.*
3. *Eat a healthy diet.* (Ideas on what constitutes a healthy diet have changed drastically, but you can get a fairly good idea from recent research.)

That's it.

Health officials in this country have come to the conclusion that too much attention has been paid to longevity and too little to preventing disease and disability, and to adding *quality* instead of mere *quantity* to the lifespan.

"Healthy People 2000" is a series of objectives set by the U.S. Public Health Service's Office of Disease Prevention and Health Promotion to improve the nation's health. One of these goals is to lengthen each adult's *functional* life, mainly through educating the public about smoking, exercise, and nutrition.

IT STARTS IN MIDDLE AGE

In many people, these "lifestyle diseases" start showing up in middle age. What do doctors see in their middle-aged patients? Decreased exercise tolerance; lower energy level and fatigue; aches and pains; chronic health conditions, such as heart disease, stroke, deteriorating eyesight, glaucoma, anxiety and stress, sleep disorders, and certain sexual changes; and psychological changes, such as depression and empty-nest syndrome; loss of self-esteem, memory, and mental agility.[5]

But the fact that physicians see so many middle-aged people exhibiting these conditions doesn't make the conditions "normal." In middle age, when some of these symptoms of our unhealthy lifestyles first appear, we have an opportunity to change the way we're living. We need all the help we can get, but very little attention is paid in this country to preventive medicine. Many people—even some doctors—feel that it's too late to change the way we live. This is simply not true.

IT'S NEVER TOO LATE TO CHANGE

All three of the common poor health practices prevalent in our culture—smoking, lack of exercise, and unhealthy diet—when changed, yield health benefits *at any age*.

Smoking, for example, is a major risk factor in eight of the top sixteen causes of death for people sixty-five and older, including emphysema, heart disease, and strokes. If you continue smoking, you are likely to spend the last years of your life on oxygen, gasping for breath, unable to walk more than a few paces. Or you may spend them undergoing painful cancer treatments, or reduced to a vegetative state by a stroke.

Even quitting smoking later in life leads to a rapid and sustained reduction in mortality from coronary heart disease.[6] However, the older smoker who is heavily addicted may need support and help in order to quit.

And just a modest increase in exercise—as little as a half hour of brisk walking per day—can help to protect you from heart disease, according to a study of 13,000 healthy people done by the Cooper Clinic in Dallas, Texas. In this group, which was followed for eight years, men who were least fit died eight times more often from heart disease and four times more often from cancer than men who were most fit. Women who were least fit died nine times more often from heart disease and sixteen times more often from cancer than their peers who were most fit.

As far as diet is concerned, Dr. Dean Ornish has proven conclusively in scientific, double-blind tests that drastically lowering the fat in the diet *reverses the disease in clogged arteries*. A typically American high-fat diet is also a risk factor in breast cancer, colon cancer, and diabetes.

If you believe, as I do, that your body is a "temple of the Holy Spirit," then you have to pay for the upkeep on the temple in a changed lifestyle.

MOVE IT EVERY DAY

Like many people who do sedentary work, I've had my share of back problems over the years. I'll never forget taking my aching shoulders and back to a chiropractor for relief and getting what must have been his standard lecture.

"Life is movement," he told me, dancing around and waving his arms for emphasis, "and movement is life! God designed our muscles to move, not to be still. You have to move them."

He was right. The less I moved, the less I was able to move. The muscles that held my back in place were weak. This chiropractor could help relieve my immediate discomfort, but long range, it was up to me to exercise to strengthen those weak muscles or I'd just get worse.

Aging bodies, like aging buildings, need more maintenance as they grow older, not less. Gradually, our body metabolism slows down—on the average 5 percent per decade. This doesn't sound like much, but the woman who used to need 2200 calories to maintain her body weight now needs only 1600. Unless she increases her activity or reduces her food intake, the excess will be stored as fat. Exercise is maintenance. Lack of use causes muscles to atrophy. Spending too much time lying in bed or lounging in front of a television set (which many retirees tend to do) will weaken the body. Weakening of the body will happen anyway unless we do something. Our bodies lose muscle mass with age. The loss will be greater unless we do something to build muscle.

Weight gains after retirement tend to make other health problems worse. Excessive weight puts a strain on your joints. If you develop osteoarthritis (a wearing down of the cartilage that often comes with age), obesity will make it worse. When people are overweight, body cells are not as receptive to the insulin that the pancreas is putting out, and adult-onset diabetes with all its problems (blindness, need for amputation of limbs due to poor circulation, etc.) can result. Excess weight puts a strain on the heart and raises the blood pressure. Often, the only treatment necessary for diabetes and high blood pressure is taking off weight, which is difficult to do with diet alone.

STRENGTH AND FLEXIBILITY NEEDED

While walking is excellent for your heart, it does little for the strength and flexibility of your other muscles. You need muscle strength to rise from a chair, climb stairs, lift grocery bags, push a vacuum cleaner. If you do nothing to maintain (or even increase) your muscle strength, you'll gradually lose the ability to do all these things. It can happen sooner than you think. One study found that 40 percent of women aged fifty-five to sixty-five could not lift even ten pounds. They were well on their way to becoming helpless and losing their independence—not from disease but from disuse.

Muscle strength also helps protect you against bone loss by increasing bone density. This reduces the risk of osteoporosis that leads to broken hips and loss of mobility in later life. In addition to strength, you need flexibility in order to protect yourself from injury. Stiffness is not inevitable with age. Exercises that stretch muscles and ligaments will keep you more supple and give you greater freedom of movement.

Conventional wisdom used to be that older people's muscles would not benefit from training. Doctors were amazed when a group of researchers at the Human Nutrition Research Center on Aging at Tufts University reported in the *Journal of the American Medical Association* that they had succeeded in strengthening the muscles of ten frail old people in a nursing home who were in their *nineties*. After training for eight weeks, these people increased muscle strength and size. Two were able to walk again without canes. But soon after the study ended, they returned to their sedentary ways and began to lose what they had gained.[7]

This study shows there is hope that many older people can avoid becoming dependent on others for their care just by making a conscious effort to become stronger. In order for this to happen, exercise has to be enjoyable and it has to be something that becomes a habit—as much a part of your daily routine as brushing your teeth.

GIVE YOURSELF TIME

This doesn't mean that you can immediately get up from your chair and start climbing mountains. People over sixty who want to start an exercise program need a doctor's okay. You need to start off slowly and increase what you do very gradually. Give yourself at least three months to begin seeing results, although you may begin feeling better almost immediately.

It won't be long before you should be tired enough to begin sleeping better. Also, exercise releases natural hormones in the brain that make you feel better. It's one of the best natural treatments for the prevention of depression, which is a very common problem for older people.

NEW NUTRITIONAL GUIDELINES

We now realize that almost everything our mothers taught us—and that we taught our children—about healthy eating was wrong, except "Eat your vegetables." A few years ago, a typical dinner at our house might have followed this pattern:

> A meat main course—six to eight ounces of red meat, or one-fourth to one-half a chicken; a baked or boiled potato swimming in butter; a small green salad, or a small portion of vegetable; pie, cake, or pudding for dessert.

I thought we were eating well. Like most Americans, I was convinced that you needed to eat large quantities of meat, which purportedly contained valuable "complete" protein. And we were also told that starches were fattening. Now the experts are saying that the opposite is true. If you want to be well-nourished and to control your weight, you need to limit the protein in your diet and increase the complex carbohydrates (which include starches).

Decreasing protein intake, especially from red meats, will automatically cut the saturated fat, cholesterol, and calories in your diet. If you eat too much protein, it's stored in the body as fat, stresses the kidneys and liver, and reduces the absorption of calcium, thus potentially leading to osteoporosis.

REDUCE FAT, INCREASE FIBER

The "normal" American diet is at least 37 percent fat, according to USDA researchers. The USDA dietary experts recommend reducing fats in your diet to 30 percent, but many medical experts believe that this is still too high, especially for people who are genetically predisposed to convert the fat they eat into cholesterol.

Increasing the fiber in your diet is recommended as a protection against high blood cholesterol, and also diseases of the colon such as diverticulitis and cancer. By getting more protein from plant rather than animal sources and by eating more fruits and vegetables, you automatically increase the amount of fiber in your diet. Eating whole grains (such as whole wheat bread, brown rice, etc.) also increases dietary fiber, and provides many additional vitamins and minerals.

Since 1956, the USDA has promoted "the basic four food groups"—meat, dairy products, fruits and vegetables, and grains—challenging us to eat something from each of the four food groups every day. In 1991, the USDA completely revised its recommendations.[8]

Forget the basic four, once diagrammed as a circle divided into four equal parts. Instead, picture a pyramid with two main food categories, grains (breads and cereals) and produce (fruits and vegetables), at the bottom, followed by progressively smaller portions of dairy products, animal protein, and fats and sweets at the top. To be healthy, according to these new USDA recommendations, we need to eat six to eleven servings from the bread, cereal, rice, and pasta group; three to five servings from the vegetable group; two to four servings from the dairy group; and two to three servings from the meat, poultry, fish, dry beans, eggs, and nuts group every day. Use fats, oils, and sweets sparingly. This is according to the most recent USDA nutritional guidelines. Almost all women's magazines and health magazines have advice for translating these recommendations into menus and recipes. Remember, these are general recommendations. Individuals differ; some have food allergies, some have diseases or take medications that influence their nutritional needs. For specific advice, see your physician or a registered dietician.

YOU ARE WHAT YOU EAT

These are not new ideas. One group of people who have not eaten a typical American diet for over a hundred years are the Seventh Day Adventists. Today, they have much lower rates of chronic "lifestyle" diseases, such as heart disease. In fact, they have half the rate of chronic lifestyle diseases of other Americans sixty-five and over. One of the founders of the Seventh Day Adventists, Mrs. Ellen G. White, taught abstinence from alcohol, tobacco, coffee, tea, and animal flesh, and stressed the importance of eating moderately from a diet based on whole grains, fruits, and vegetables.

Mrs. White was preaching a return to a "biblical diet." While it's difficult to argue from biblical evidence that the Israelites were vegetarians, whole grains played a much more important role in their diet than they do in most Americans' diets today. Medical science, which started out scoffing at Mrs. White's ideas, now is forced by the evidence to come around much closer to her way of thinking.

ENJOYABLE, HEALTHY EATING

However, it's one thing to adopt this diet with the support of a church community behind you and another to try to do it on your own. How radically do you have to change the way you eat in order to prevent some of these chronic diseases?

Remember, this way of eating is not a "diet" for you to go off and back on at will. If you change your eating pattern to prevent chronic diseases, you will have to eat this way for the rest of your life. And unless food tastes good, you probably won't continue to do so.

Over the past few years, we have totally changed the way we eat at our house. We don't miss our former way of eating at all. In fact, we like the new way better because it's so delicious.

For one thing, there is more variety. Vegetable sources of protein include all kinds of legumes (peas and beans), and whole grains, such as wheat, rye, barley, corn, millet, and rice. Trying out these new foods has meant dipping into all the cuisines of the world—Oriental stir fries, Mexican dishes based on corn tortillas with beans, Indian curries, Thai satays, Middle Eastern vegetable stews with couscous, Italian pastas, etc. All of these cuisines use small quantities of meat, poultry, and fish as flavoring rather than as the main part of the meal.

These cuisines are not only nutritious and delicious, but also very filling. You can eat larger quantities of them than of the typical American meal without gaining weight. And you don't have to give up your favorite recipes. New cookbooks will show you how to reduce the fat and make the old recipes healthier.

MAKE CHANGES GRADUALLY

However, I've made changes very slowly over a period of several years. You can begin by substituting—skim milk for whole milk in recipes, nonfat yogurt for sour cream—and reducing the sugar and fat in your regular recipes.

If you suddenly eliminate salt, food tastes blah. But if you gradually reduce the salt, you adapt to the change without even noticing it. If you switch suddenly to nonfat milk, it tastes like water. But if you go from whole milk to 2 percent fat to 1 percent fat to nonfat over a period of months, you will adapt more easily.

Then you can start reducing the meat portions and increasing the vegetable portions of your meals. Have a vegetarian meal based on beans or pasta one day a week, then two, then three. If you suddenly increase the amount of fiber that you're eating, you'll probably suffer from digestive disturbances. You have to give your body time to adjust.

HOW AM I DOING?

It's easy to believe you're eating right, but difficult to know if your meals are meeting your nutritional goals. To satisfy my curiosity, I recently had a consultation with Elaine Groen, a registered dietician who has had years of experience working with seniors at a nearby retirement community.

I kept track of everything I ate for a week, and sent five days of menus to her. She fed the information for three of those days into her computer, which has a program for analyzing the nutritional content.

At our meeting, she gave me a printout that showed the amounts of each of almost fifty nutrients in a column. Next to that column was the USDA's Recommended Daily Allowance (RDA), and a third column showing my intake as a percentage of the RDA. I was pleased to see that our new way of eating was more than meeting my nutritional needs, with the exception of calcium. I need (and am taking) a supplement to bring that up to the recommended 1200 to 1500 milligrams per day to help prevent osteoporosis (brittle bones) in post-menopausal women.

DO YOU NEED SUPPLEMENTS?

People over sixty are the largest consumers of nutritional supplements in this country, but much of the money they spend is wasted. The American Council on Science and Health, a nonprofit consumer education organization, estimates that health frauds, including nutritional supplements, cost unsuspecting seniors an estimated $10 billion a year.

You'll frequently see "miracle" anti-aging nutrients touted in advertising or written about in magazine articles. There is no known substance that slows aging and extends life, says the National Institute on Aging. Megadosing on vitamins and minerals is not only wasteful, it can also be dangerous.

Everybody needs selenium (a mineral), but only in minute amounts. Too much (and it doesn't take much to be too much) is poisonous. You can also poison yourself with overdoses of Vitamin A. Too much B^6 can cause nerve damage. A popular book recommends high doses of niacin (a B vitamin) to lower blood cholesterol. While it's true that niacin lowers blood cholesterol, what the ads for this vitamin don't tell you is that it also can damage your liver. If you take it, you need to be under a doctor's supervision and have your liver enzymes checked regularly.

What those who tout mineral supplements for seniors don't tell you is that taking a single mineral can upset the body's mineral balance, says Judith Hall Frisch, Ph.D., senior staff fellow at the National Institute on Aging. Too much zinc, for example, interferes with the absorption of copper.

RDAs are not *minimum* amounts. Actually, they're set well above what would be needed to prevent disease in younger people. But no RDAs have been set for people over fifty, and preliminary research indicates that nutritional needs do change as we age. Exactly how they change still needs more investigation.

SAFE SUPPLEMENTS

"Those [seniors] with certain medical conditions do need supplements," says James Davis, M.D., of the Department of Geriatrics, UCLA Medical School. "Some groups at risk nutritionally include alcoholics, those with chronic illnesses that interfere with appetite, those who are living alone or who are cognitively impaired (such as Alzheimer's patients) and those who take certain medications."

For example, aspirin taken for arthritis may deplete the body of iron. Diuretics can cause a loss of potassium and other minerals. NSAIDs (non-steroid anti-inflammatory drugs) and Dilantin can rob the bones of calcium. Ask your doctor about what he recommends for supplements if you take any of these medications.

Some recent experiments performed at the Human Research

Center on Aging and Nutrition at Tufts University strongly indicate that Vitamins A, B^6, C, and E play a role in preventing cancer and cardiovascular disease by boosting the body's natural immunity. But this does not mean that seniors should take large doses of any of these, says Dr. Jeffrey Blumberg, who has directed some of these studies.

If you eat properly, you may already be getting all you need. Elaine's printout, for example, showed that even without any vitamin pill, I was getting 249 percent of the RDA of Vitamin A and 211 percent of the RDA of Vitamin C from my food. (There is no stated RDA for Vitamin E.)

Both Dr. Blumberg and other experts I've consulted recommend a safe, sane, balanced approach. You can get all the protection you need by taking a single multi-vitamin and mineral pill once a day—*in addition* to a sound diet, not instead of it. Anything more than that is risky unless a doctor has determined that you have a deficiency.

OLD AGE IS NOT A DIAGNOSIS

If you adopt a healthy diet, exercise, and don't smoke, you are less likely to experience many of the chronic diseases of the aging—*but* this is no guarantee of perfect health. Genetics and unknown causes of disease are also at work. In addition, the likelihood increases with age of suffering from such conditions as insomnia, depression, dementia, impotence, incontinence, and other ills, all of which are either treatable or may be symptoms of diseases that can be treated.

Unfortunately, too many doctors take the attitude, "What can you expect at your age?" This is not acceptable, so don't accept it. Get a second opinion; ask for a referral to a specialist.

Some of these conditions can also be caused by the medications that doctors prescribe. An important part of preventive self-care as you age is protecting yourself against mismedication and over-medication, caused either by yourself or by doctors.

DRUGS AND THE AGING BODY

While people over sixty make up only 17 percent of the U.S. population, they account for more than half of all people hospitalized for drug-related problems each year. People over sixty are four times more likely to die from a drug reaction than the younger population, according to a 1990 report by the U.S. Inspector General. Over 50,000 patients per year suffer from drug-induced dementias (senility), and 32,000 per year lose their independence after suffering from drug-induced falls.

The more drugs you're taking, the greater the potential danger. One group of researchers found that the older person who takes four to five pills daily is three times more likely to suffer an adverse reaction than the person who takes two to three pills, including over-the-counter pills that you can buy without a prescription.

Helen Levens Lipton, Ph.D., and Philip R. Lee, M.D., of the University of California at San Francisco, who have studied this problem for over ten years, place a lot of blame on doctors. Aging kidneys and livers become less efficient at removing drugs from the body. So doctors should prescribe lower dosages for their older patients, but frequently they don't.

Doctors sometimes are unknowingly treating the side effects of medication with more medication instead of discontinuing the offending drug. Depression, for example, is a common side effect of some blood pressure and heart medicines. Yet some doctors will either ignore the patient's complaints or put him on antidepressant drugs. This is how people sometimes end up in nursing homes with drug-induced dementias.

Patients sometimes create part of the problem by failing to take their medication correctly. Or they may take each of their symptoms to a different specialist and end up with a collection of different drugs, some of which may have terrible consequences when taken together.

It's important to have one primary care physician who reviews all the medications you're taking. Make sure he or she keeps you informed. Have all your prescriptions filled at one pharmacy, which keeps a computerized record of everything you're taking. This way, the pharmacist can spot potentially dangerous drug combinations. If you have a question about the drugs you're taking, your pharmacist is an excellent source of information. If your doctor won't listen to you about a problem you're having with a prescription drug, ask your pharmacist some questions. Perhaps he would be willing to call the doctor.

If you have a bad reaction to a drug, be assertive with your physician. There is almost always an alternative drug you can be taking that may not have the same side effects for *you*.

YOU HAVE A RIGHT TO KNOW:
QUESTIONS TO ASK YOUR DOCTOR ABOUT DRUGS

"Don't let doctors put you off with Medspeak," says Barry Levin, a consulting pharmacist. "It's your right to have your questions about medications answered in a way you'll understand."

Ask: What is the name of the medication I'm taking? What is it supposed to do? (In other words, Why am I taking it?) Has a firm diagnosis been established?

What would happen if I didn't take it?

What's the smallest dose I can get by with?

Exactly how should I take it—amount, number of times per day, time of day, with or without food, any foods I should avoid eating while on this medication?

Don't trust your memory. Write all this down.

Keep a list of all the medications you're taking in a place where it will be accessible in an emergency.

GETTING THE HELP YOU NEED

Where can you find the help you need to get started on a suitable diet and exercise program?

- Many hospitals have what they call "wellness" programs, and many of those are specifically geared for seniors. Call your local hospital's community education department. Their services may include advice from registered dieticians, exercise classes, sometimes even weight machines and training experts.
- YMCAs and health clubs will design a program for you or get you into an exercise group of people your age.
- Most senior centers include exercise classes as part of their program. Some also have classes on nutrition.
- Arthritis Foundation classes of water exercise are found in many communities. Exercise in a swimming pool is excellent for rehabilitating osteoarthritis sufferers. The water supports your weight, and you are able to move without straining your joints. People who couldn't even get into the pool without help have been able, in a few months time, to walk again unaided.
- Everybody can walk without a special program. I know—

it's often hard to make yourself do it alone. So get a dog that needs exercise. This will help motivate you. Or walk with a friend or spouse. Join a group at your senior center. Go mall walking. Many malls throughout the country have started this activity for seniors. It's ideal when walking outdoors isn't possible because the neighborhood is unsafe or the weather is too severe.

LIGHTEN UP!

One final word: Good health habits are not a substitute religion, nor are they a charm to ward off death.

I showed my husband an announcement I saw in a church bulletin: "Join our exercise class. Statistics prove that fitness reduces the mortality rate."

"That's absurd!" I said. "The mortality rate is the same for everybody; it's 100 percent. Nobody gets out of this world alive."

"They mean the mortality rate at each age level," he said.

"Oh."

That still doesn't impress me. I'm content to leave the number of years that I spend on this planet to God. But my health while I'm in this body is at least partially up to me. What He gave me is *my* responsibility to maintain. And a healthy body will make anybody's old age more enjoyable—not just for you but for the family that might otherwise have to take care of you.

QUESTIONS FOR DISCUSSION

1. What lifestyle changes do you need to make?
2. Can you join a group or form a partnership with someone who will help keep you motivated and accountable?
3. What further steps will you take to educate yourself on exercise, and planning and cooking healthy meals?
4. Can you answer all the questions listed in the box "You Have a Right to Know" about each of the medications you're currently taking (including nonprescription drugs)?
5. Do you have a primary care physician you feel comfortable communicating with?

CHAPTER TWENTY-ONE

STRENGTHENING YOUR SPIRITUAL MUSCLES

He has saved the best for last.
Jane M. Thibault

An older woman named Catherine came to Jane M. Thibault for counseling because she seemed to have everything, yet she wasn't happy.

"I have a feeling that there's more to life than I have experienced. I don't know what that is, but I crave it and nothing else will satisfy me. I think my problem is that I just can't get in touch with what that 'something more' is. I'm so frustrated," Catherine said.

Catherine's quest for something more that she had not yet experienced is related to the questions that old people often raise: "What good am I? What is old age for?"

The belief that there must be some meaning to old age—even though this meaning may elude us—is a common one. Is it true, as the book of Ecclesiastes says, that God "has made everything beautiful in its time" (Ecclesiastes 3:11)? Then what is the beauty of old age? If the physical body is all there is, then when that goes, argue the euthanasia enthusiasts, the only sensible solution is to take the quickest exit possible. And of course, if the physical body is all there is, they're right.

But most of us know in our heart of hearts that the physical body is not all there is. So, what is this "something more"?

Thibault comments, "Catherine may be typical of the older adult Christian who finds herself in a state of emptiness. . . . She had led a good, useful Christian life, but this life was oriented to the external aspects of her religion. This dedicated woman truly loved God, but her love was a discipline of her will. She had not yet 'fallen in love' with her God."[1]

The opportunity to encounter God as *Lover* is the special opportunity—the "something more"—of later life, Thibault believes. God has saved the best for last.

EXTERIOR VERSUS INTERIOR SUPPORT

Like Catherine, many of us may have been brought up in religious traditions that give lip service to having a personal relationship with God. But in practice, they simply place an emphasis on behaving in a correct or moral manner. These are *externals—doing* rather than *being*.

"I've tried to do the right thing all my life," some older people say, "and now I have cancer." Underlying this comment are the unspoken false beliefs, "I deserve better!" and, "Now that I can no longer 'do' for God, I must be worthless."

The supports of *external* religion are no longer working. In our final years, only our *internal* supports really matter, and they may be quite weak from lack of exercise. At retirement, you will have ample time to strengthen your spiritual muscles, if you choose to do so.

But why bother?

Because if we don't learn to grow spiritually, our natural self-centeredness will grow stronger with age. We all know old people who create a living hell for themselves and anyone unfortunate enough to be around them. They focus their attention on their aches and pains, worrying constantly about their health, and they complain when things don't go their way. I don't want to be like that. Do you?

COPING WITH THE INEVITABLE

Old age is very stressful. No matter how well we've taken care of ourselves, physical illness may strike. We will all have losses to bear—of spouse, and friends, and physical strength.
How will we cope?

We may enter the last years of our lives with mainly *negative* coping strategies: numbing our pain with drugs or alcohol, overeating, excessive television watching, blaming others for our problems, blowing our stacks, or repressing our feelings deep inside.

What are some positive coping strategies we may need to learn? In addition to physical exercise, the positive strategies are all spiritual in nature: communicating with God through prayer, talking things over with a friend or confidant, writing in a journal, and especially, developing the habit of praise.

This last item may not be so easy.

All your life, you may have avoided facing anything unpleasant, and you may not know how to handle the grief that accompanies the inevitable losses of old age. From the groundbreaking work of Elisabeth Kubler-Ross (author of *On Death and Dying*), we learn that grieving typically has five stages: denial, anger, bargaining, depression, and acceptance. Many older people become "stuck" in anger or depression, unable to move on to acceptance. The only tools that are really going to help are spiritual tools.

HOW DO WE LEARN?

How did Jane Thibault help Catherine learn to use these spiritual tools to discover her "something more"? By acting as her mentor, teaching her how to pray in ways that would help her draw closer to God.

By the time you reach retirement, your need to have mentors in your business and professional life is probably over, but your need to have spiritual mentors—never!

Pastor Ron Lee Davis describes the process of finding mentors. Since so many spiritual lessons are "caught" rather than taught, Pastor Davis was fortunate in having his father, also a pastor, as his first mentor. As he looks back, he recognizes that mentors sometimes "just happened" to come into his life, and at other times he consciously sought them out.

"The first ingredient a learner must bring to a mentoring relationship is his own emptiness, his teachability," Pastor Davis writes. "Just as it the empty volume within a cup that makes it useful, it is the empty volume within us that enables us as learners to receive from our mentors and to be useful to God."[2]

SEEKING MENTORS

Every major world religion has spread its teachings through the use of mentors. In the Catholic tradition, those who want to go deeper into their faith seek out a "spiritual master" or "soul friend"—someone more advanced spiritually who meets with them regularly, teaches them methods of prayer, answers their questions, and monitors their progress. This has not been a common practice in modern Protestantism. Perhaps it needs to be revived.

A mentor need not be a chronologically older person. When she was a new Christian in her forties, says my friend Grace, her mentor was a twenty-two-year-old. However, I believe that it's vitally important to seek out spiritually mature older people and learn from them.

We are all apprentices to the aging. We are going to places where none but the old have ever gone before. The old have special spiritual needs we know little about. We will need those who've gone before us as guides—which is, of course, one of the meanings of the word "mentor" (other meanings are trusted counselor, coach, and teacher).

HOPE OR DESPAIR?

In the past, little attention was paid to the spiritual needs of older people. Is it because we believe, as many secular gerontologists do, that the old have no future?

Christian writer Dorothy L. Sayers had a different perspective: "Paradoxical as it may seem, to believe in youth is to look backward. To look forward, we must believe in age."

Some find their future and their hope by turning their thoughts toward heaven. Grace, who is one of my mentors, says, "Now when it's no longer possible for me to get out and hike in the mountains, I remember their beauty. Then I think about the beauty I'm going to experience in heaven that's going to be so much more beautiful than anything I've known on earth. That comforts me."

As older persons, we can find joy in mentoring younger generations, knowing that we will live on in their deeds and thoughts. "Even in death, we mentors are immortal," Davis says.[3]

Without this perspective, it's all too easy for elderly people to fall into despair. "What did I live for?" is a question that we can no longer avoid. Mentoring gives us a sense of accomplishment in our advanced years.

LIFE AS A SPIRITUAL JOURNEY

It is a logical thing to ask yourself when you reach your senior years, "What has been the meaning and purpose of my life?" The best help in answering that question awaits you within your own memories. Do you see your life as a spiritual journey?

There's an old saying: "God gave us memory so that we could have roses in December." In Dostoevski's novel *The Brothers Karamazov*, the saintly Alyosha has something relevant to say to us about the value of cherished memories:

> You must know that there is nothing higher and stronger and more wholesome and good for life in the future than some good memory, especially a memory of childhood, of home. People talk to you a great deal about your education, but some good, sacred memory, preserved from childhood, is perhaps the best education. If one carries many such memories into life, one is safe to the end of one's days.

But it's not just the good memories that are life affirming. If our life has really been a spiritual journey, even the so-called "bad" memories are part of the pattern that gives our lives meaning. Somehow, we need to look at the bad memories, too, and be able to say triumphantly, "With God's help, I survived!" Somehow, if we are to reach acceptance, we must be able to say, "These things helped shape me into the person I am."

DISCOVERING MEANINGS

Kirk Dewey, who was ninety-three when he wrote his life story, recalled an incident that took place when he was an Iowa farm boy. He'd been left in charge of his younger sister one day when his parents went into town to do some shopping. While they were gone, Kirk accidentally broke his mother's favorite vase. All afternoon, he was miserable.

When his parents came home, he blurted out what had happened. This is what he wrote: "My mother sank down right there in the dusty farmyard, and took me on her lap. I'll never forget how she threw her arms around me and held me close. 'Oh, you dear little boy; have you been worrying about that all afternoon?' She hugged me tight. I felt the warmth of her love, and everything was all right after all. And that's how I learnt about forgiveness."[4]

The last sentence states quite well the *meaning* of that particular chapter of this man's life. Spiritual autobiography is your life story—*plus* interpretation. It answers the question, "What was God doing in my life through this incident?"

Through this process of looking back at your life, you get to know yourself a little better. You also get to know God better as you begin to recognize His presence throughout your life.

There are two approaches you could use in writing your life story: (1) Start with a list of topics, such as love, faith, prayer, shame, anger, etc., then try to recall experiences reflecting those qualities. (2) Start with the specific experiences that you remember, and then try to discover what these memories mean to you. Nobody else can do this for you, but other people can help you do it.

THE NEED FOR HELPERS

Thinking about your life experiences in your mind without telling them to another human being is just not the same as writing them down for someone else to read, as Dan Wakefield points out. One of the students in his spiritual autobiography course said, "What I found is I could write something and read it to myself and it would probably have little impact, but if I'm with someone else and read it aloud, there's something about another person's presence that makes it 'ring true.' It's much more powerful."[5] There is something about the reaction of other people that validates your experiences and stimulates you to remember more.

Ideally, this is best done in a group devoted to spiritual autobiography. It need not necessarily be restricted to a group of older people. Spiritual autobiography can be done at any age. All that's required is a sympathetic teacher and a group of no more than eight to ten like-minded, supportive people. Wakefield suggests the church community as an ideal setting for such a class. However, you don't have to join a class. Two people who meet together regularly to share their life stories and encourage each other would be enough.

THE GOSPEL AS STORY

As we advance in age, failing vision and hearing may make it difficult for us to read or hear the Word of God the way we used to. How fortunate, then, are those who have committed parts of the Bible to memory. There are many comforting passages of Scripture that I could recommend. But in addition, Thomas E. Boomershine, Professor of New Testament at United Theological Seminary in Dayton, Ohio, and founder of the Network of Biblical Storytellers, suggests committing entire stories from the gospels to memory. The purpose is not just to tell them to others (although that is important), but to tell them to ourselves.

Boomershine, a professional storyteller, had committed the story of Jesus' healing of the paralytic in Mark 2:1-13 to memory. He was hit by an automobile and spent six months in casts. It was doubtful if he would ever walk again. During that period, the story of the healing of the paralytic became *his* story.

> I began telling it to myself during the physical therapy in the hospital. . . . But the most frequent tellings were during the months of physical therapy at home. . . . Sometimes it was a story of hope. I would often envision myself getting up and walking again. Often it was a story of forgiveness. . . . It was a story which gave me a context for exploring my skepticism about ever being able to walk again and about God's ability to enable me to do that. All of my critical and cynical energies as a scholar found expression in the scribes' questions.
>
> Day by day, in a variety of ways, I told myself this story and remembered it in exquisite detail. Writing in my journal, prayer and doing my exercises all became occasions for remembering this story. And in an equally varied numbers of ways, the story enabled me to recognize and accept Jesus' presence and power. In the process of remembering this story, Jesus Christ became present to me.[6]

In his book entitled *Story Journey*, Boomershine gives numerous examples of the healing power of gospel stories told to others at difficult and stressful points in their lives. It's an approach I'm eager to put into practice.

SPIRITUAL DISCIPLINES

"Discipline" is a castor oil sort of word to most people. Yet the true meaning of discipline is not punishment, but training. "God has given us the Disciplines of the spiritual life as a means of receiving his grace. The Disciplines allow us to place ourselves before God so that he can transform us."[7]

Richard Foster, whose book *Celebration of Discipline* has become, since its first publication in 1978, a modern classic, names eight disciplines for the individual: meditation, prayer, fasting, study, simplicity, solitude, submission, and service; and four corporate disciplines: confession, worship, guidance, and celebration. It's impossible to learn these disciplines from a book; you learn them by doing them, preferably under the guidance of a mentor. (However, I strongly recommend that you do get a book on spiritual disciplines and learn more about them.)

Three disciplines that I'd especially like to focus on for older people are meditation, solitude, and prayer.

MEDITATION

"Be still, and know that I am God" does not come naturally to our hyperactive culture. Our minds are such squirrel cages of incessant activity that it will require practice to stop thinking our own thoughts and be still long enough for God to get through to us. Yet in advancing years, when we are forced to slow down, if we have learned to meditate we can focus our minds on God instead of on our own negative, self-defeating thoughts.

Modern Christians are largely unaware that a long tradition of Christian meditation exists. Christian meditation is not, Foster insists, a kind of psychological manipulation that will drop our blood pressure (although this may well happen as a side effect.) "If you believe in a universe created by the infinite-personal God who delights in our communion with him, you will see meditation as communication between the Lover and the one beloved."[8]

As the authors of the book *The Golden Years, Riding the Crest* say, "Christian meditation is not something strange. . . . In fact, we all know how to meditate already! We did it as children anticipating what was in the big box under the Christmas tree. . . . We did it as a parent, wondering about our children. We did it as a worker, pondering how to do our job better."[9]

In most Bible study, we are looking for an abstract "meaning." In meditation, through the use of a sanctified sense of wonder, we are accepting and pondering a personal message.

One starting point for meditation could be something from the created order: a tree, a plant, a bird. What does God show us of Himself in this aspect of His creation? Examples of this type of prayer/meditation can be found in *Praying Our Goodbyes* by Joyce Rupp, and in chapter 9, "Seven Spiritual Exercises for Wide-Awake Nights," of Connie Soth's book *Insomnia, God's Night School*. Neither of these was originally intended for older adults, but both are applicable.

LONELINESS OR SOLITUDE?

If we're going to be spending more time alone as we age, we have a choice. We can choose to be lonely, *or* we can embrace the spiritual discipline of solitude. Foster also says, "Loneliness is inner emptiness. Solitude is inner fulfillment."[10] But most of us need to learn how to be alone without feeling lonely. Then we will also learn that God meets us best in solitude when all other distractions have been removed.

Every retiree should consider deliberately seeking opportunities for solitude—retreats, mini-vacations from other people, appointments to be alone with God. One resourceful woman found just such an opportunity for solitude through a very common complaint of the older years: insomnia.

"GOD'S NIGHT SCHOOL"

More than half of all people over sixty-five complain about insomnia, but few recognize it as a spiritual opportunity. Worn out from battling sleeplessness, one night Connie Soth decided to get up, accept the "friendly silence" of her sleeping household, and ask God to show her what He wanted to teach her. She began searching the Scriptures and recording her observations in her "Midnight Journal." The sleep that had eluded her when she demanded it now came unbidden more often than not. But what she found was much more than a "cure" for insomnia. She writes,

> Then something new began to happen. A few hours into the night I would wake up as though to the ring of an alarm—but not the one ticking on the nightstand. This silent signal, I learned, meant that I should leave my bed and bring my Bible and my midnight journal

> to the dining room table. . . . He wants to teach each of us to listen in the silent night and to say, "Speak, Lord, for your servant listens."[11]

Connie found, as all seekers can, something more important than sleep. Being alone with God in the middle of the night, when all the daytime distractions are far away, can give us the opportunity to do some of the important spiritual work of the later years. It may be the cleansing of unconfessed sins of the past, forgiving others and asking forgiveness for ourselves, or bringing to mind those with whom we need to seek reconciliation and healing of relationships. It may be learning to simply "be" with Him, bathing ourselves in the light of His love.

There is much more to prayer than most of us have ever dreamed possible, and now we have great volumes of time to learn it.

One person who learned this lesson at a relatively young age is Carol Long, a tall, slim, beautiful woman in her sixties. Her face is radiant beneath a cap of smartly styled silver hair.

Carol had been a busy person all her life. She was secretary to the senior pastor of a large church and an active crafts hobbyist. The mother of four children and grandmother of seven, Carol had been taking care of one child still at home, her elderly father, and her invalid husband when illness struck *her* in 1989. The diagnosis: ovarian cancer, the same disease that had claimed the lives of her mother and her sister.

INTIMACY WITH GOD

"It was like a shock of cold water hitting my face," Carol said. "I was forced to face my own mortality, to put things in order with my children and my grandchildren—and with God whom I'd taken for granted all these years."

Carol's prognosis was grave. Although doctors did not hold out much hope, she decided on radical surgery, followed by chemotherapy. Four months after her surgery, her husband died.

The recovery process for Carol was difficult and slow. Her church helped with meals, transportation, and prayer—human support that was indispensable. But even more important to Carol was the closeness to God that she developed through her suffering. "I turned my life around," Carol said. "I thought I was a spiritual person before this happened, but now I know I wasn't really. My former prayer life was superficial."

Following surgery, she was too weak to do anything but lie on the couch in her living room and pray. Others from church came, kneeling and praying with her.

As she gained strength, her prayer life expanded. Intercessory prayer for others (with the aid of a prayer notebook for recording requests) is now her chief purpose in life. She spends one hour in the morning and one hour in the evening in prayer, and an additional hour in Bible study. She holds a weekly prayer meeting in her home. Gradually, by learning to husband her strength, she's been able to add some outside activities. But her life will never return to what it was before.

What's she's given up is nothing, Carol says, compared with what she's gained in intimacy with God.

"I can now say, 'Thank You, God, for this affliction that You've given me,'" Carol said. "I'm so grateful for this time. I doubt that I'd ever have gotten to this point without it."

USING SUFFERING CREATIVELY

Nobody would ask for cancer as a means of getting closer to God. But if it happens to us, Carol's story gives us hope to help us work through our grief and pain to a new spiritual height that we could not have reached before. Carol's sense of acceptance is something that could never take place as a matter of course.

Keeping a prayer notebook as Connie Soth did could be a vital aid in helping us work through various stages of anger, frustration, and depression. Being honest before God in our prayer life really helps the healing process. A prayer notebook will also help us learn to know ourselves better, and to record how God has been at work in our lives.

Part of the wisdom of age is the realization that even suffering can be a necessary part of our growth process. "Suffering is beneficial," writes Joyce Rupp, "when it leads to some kind of 'resurrection' in us, when a strength or a sleeping energy is aroused, when talents heretofore unknown are recognized, when a clarity about life's purpose and direction becomes keener for us, when a stronger sense of compassion for others deepens within us. There is so much within us that needs to come to life."[12]

Our physical powers may *need* to fade before our spiritual powers can grow. Our culture says that suffering should not exist, and that old age is a tragedy. But old age is not a tragedy. A life without meaning is a tragedy. Dying without knowing God is a tragedy. That's the only thing we need to fear. Suffering can lead us back to God. He is the only one who can extend our "final years" into a glorious eternity.

QUESTIONS FOR DISCUSSION

1. What areas of your own spiritual life need work?
2. Is the time right for you to start your own spiritual autobiography? Is there another person or an interested group you could join?
3. Do you have a spiritual mentor? Is there someone you're mentoring?

APPENDIX
RESOURCES AND FURTHER READING

Chapter Three: Planning to Grow

Bianchi, Eugene C. *Aging as a Spiritual Journey*. New York: Crossroad, 1989.

Boursma, William. "Christian Adulthood." *Adulthood*, ed. Erik Erikson. New York: Norton, 1978.

Comfort, Alex. *Say Yes to Old Age*. New York: Crown Books, 1990 (first published 1976, as *A Good Age*).

Episcopal Society of Ministry on Aging, ed. *Affirmative Aging*. Minneapolis, MN: Winston Press, 1985.

Whitehead, E.E. and J.D. *Christian Life Patterns*. New York: Doubleday, 1979.

Chapter Four: Time for Exploration and Discovery

Willig, Jules Z. *The Reality of Retirement: The Inner Experience of Becoming a Retired Person*. New York: Wm. Morrow & Co., 1981.

Chapter Five: Volunteering: Finding Yourself by Giving Yourself Away

ACTION administers VISTA (Volunteers in Service to America), RSVP (Retired Service Volunteer Program), Foster Grandparents Program, and Senior Companion Program, 806 Connecticut Ave. N.W., Washington, DC 20525 (1-800-424-8580). These federal government-sponsored programs offer a variety of opportunities in all areas of the United States.

American Hiking Society Helping Out, 1015 - 31st St. N.W., Washington, DC 20007. Send $5 for an annual directory of volunteer opportunities in U.S. national parks, national forests, and state parks.

Beatitudes Center, 555 W. Glendale Ave., Phoenix, AZ 85021, uses volunteers for a wide range of services to the elderly.

Chambré, Susan Maizen. *Good Deeds in Old Age: Volunteering by the New Leisure Class*. Lexington, MA: Lexington Books, 1987.

Ecumenical Convalescent Hospital Ministry of Marin, P.O. Box 2447, San Rafael, CA 94912, offers innovative programs and materials.

Generations United, the National Council on the Aging, 409 Third St. S.W., Washington, DC 20034, an organization that links intergenerational networks in states throughout the U.S. It should be able to direct you to local groups and programs. Also from NCOA: additional information on Family Friends and Teamwork programs.

Global Volunteers, 375 E. Little Canada Rd., St. Paul, MN 55117, arranges work trips in cooperation with local host groups around the world.

Habitat for Humanity, 419 W. Church St., Americus, GA 31709, builds housing for the poor. There are chapters throughout the U.S.

Intercristo, the Christian Career Specialists, 19303 Fremont Ave. N., Seattle, WA 98133-3800, deals mainly with paid positions, but also finds opportunities for those who raise their own support. Intercristo charges a fee for services.

Literacy Volunteers of America, 5795 Widewaters Pkw., Syracuse, NY 13214, teaches adults to read. (Call Contact Literacy Center, 1-800-228-8813; or contact your local library.)

Mobile Assistance Program, 1736 N. Sierra Bonita Ave., Pasadena, CA 91104, sends out teams to work on church building and repair projects.

National Council on the Aging, 409 Third St. N.W., Washington, DC 20024, focuses on various projects. For example, Family Friends trains older volunteers to help young persons with chronic illness or disability; Discovery Through the Humanities sponsors local discussion groups for seniors in literature and local history.

National Federation of Interfaith Volunteer Caregivers, 105 Mary's Ave., P.O. Box 1939, Kingston, NY 12401, sponsors volunteers who serve the elderly. They have chapters in various U.S. locales and offer information on setting up a ministry.

National Retiree Volunteer Center, 607 Marquette Ave., Suite 10, Minneapolis, MN 55402, targets various projects.

Older Adult Ministry, A Resource for Program Development, Presbyterian Publishing House, 341 Ponce de Leon Ave. N.E., Atlanta, GA 30365, contains ideas for local congregations.

Parish Social Ministries for Older Adults, Archdiocesan Office of Urban Affairs (Catholic), 81 Saltonstall Ave., New Haven, CT 06513, a manual for congregations. Many other denominations have intergenerational projects and resources through their committees on aging or educational centers.

Peace Corps, Washington, DC 20526 (1-800-424-8580), offers opportunities around the world for older people with skills to share.

St. James Church Social Care Program, 2942 South Wabash St., Chicago, Il 60616, has an active ministry of church members volunteering with elderly poor.

SCORE (Service Corps of Retired Executives), 1825 Connecticut Ave. N.W., Suite 503, Washington, DC 20009 (1-800-368-5855), provides free counseling for small business people. A local chapter may be listed in your phone book.

Senior Citizen School Volunteer Program: A Manual for Program Implementation, Generations Together, U. of Pittsburgh, the Center for the Study of Aging, 700 Madison Ave., Albany, NY 12208. (The Center has a free catalog of other books on intergenerational topics and on aging in general.)

Shepherd's Centers of America, 6700 Troost Ave., Suite 616, Kansas City, MO 64118, helps churches set up local volunteer ministries to the elderly.

Tobin, Sheldon S., et al. *Enabling the Elderly: Religious Institutions Within the Community Service System.* Albany, NY: State U. of New York Press, 1986.

Veterans Hospitals, as well as other hospitals, always need volunteers. Tasks vary. Contact the director of volunteers at your local hospital.

VITA (Volunteers in Technical Assistance), 1915 North Lynn St., Suite 200, Arlington, VA 22209, provides opportunities in "developing nations" around the world.

Volunteer: The Comprehensive Guide to Voluntary Service in the U.S. and Abroad, 1990–1991 edition ($6.95), Adrienne Downey ed., Council on International Education Exchange Commission on Voluntary Service and Action (CIEE), 205 E. 42nd, New York, NY 10017. This valuable guide lists agencies that offer volunteer opportunities. You can then contact the agencies for more information.

Chapter Six: Education and Travel Are Wasted on the Young

Arthur Frommer's New World of Travel. New York: Prentice-Hall (revised annually). Summer camps for adults and campus educational vacations are listed.

Council on International Educational Exchange. *Work Study Travel Abroad: The Whole World Handbook.* New York: St. Martin's Press (revised annually). This handbook is geared more toward college-age youth, but it's full of ideas, as well as resources to contact.

Elderhostel, 75 Federal St., Boston, MA 02110.

Heilman, Joan Rattner. *Unbelievably Good Deals & Great Adventures That You Absolutely Can't Get Unless You're Over 50.* Chicago: Contemporary Books, 1988. Retirement centers and educational and camping opportunities are listed in chapters 15 and 16.

Institute for Lifetime Learning, 1909 K St. N.W., Washington, DC 20009, offers two useful booklets: *Tuition Policies in Higher Education for Older Adults*—a rundown on fee waivers or reduced fees, and *College Centers for Older Learners*—a state-by-state list of learning programs for older adults.

North Carolina Center for Creative Retirement, U. of North Carolina at Asheville, Ashville, NC 28804-3299.

Official Guide to Christian Camps and Conference Centers, Christian Camping International, P.O. Box 646, Wheaton, IL 60189, contains information on church-sponsored camps and summer workshops.

Chapter Seven: If You Need Paid Employment

AARP'S Worker Equity Department, 1909 K St. N.W., Washington, DC 20049, provides a variety of career assessment and planning aids for workers. NOWIS (National Older Workers Information System) has a computerized databank of older worker employment programs available for employers.

Displaced Homemakers Network, 1010 Vermont Ave. N.W., Washington, DC 20005, helps older women who are forced into the job market by widowhood or divorce.

Forty Plus, 1718 P St. N.W., Washington, DC 20036, sponsors job clubs for middle-aged and older workers in many U.S. cities.

Operation ABLE headquarters, 180 N. Wabash Ave., Suite 802, Chicago, IL 60601 (1-312-782-3335).

Senior Career Planning & Placement Service, 257 Park Ave. S., New York, NY 10010 (1-212-529-6660), finds full-time or part-time management spots for retired executives all over the country. Send them your résumé.

For help with consulting and home businesses:

American Association of Professional Consultants, 9140 Ward Pkw., Kansas City, MO 64114 (1-816-444-3500).

Brabec, Barbara. *Homemade Money* (book), and *National Home Business Report* (newsletter), P.O. Box 2137, Naperville, IL 60566, are full of useful information.

Edwards, Paul and Sarah. *Working from Home: Everything You Need to Know About Living and Working Under the Same Roof.* Los Angeles, CA: Jeremy P. Tarcher, 1985. As consultants in home-based businesses, the authors have written a helpful book.

National Alliance of Homebased Businesswomen, P.O. Box 95, Norwood, NJ 07648.

Snelling, Lauraine. *Start Your Own Business After 50 – or 60 – or 70!* San Leandro, CA: Bristol Publishing, 1990.

Chapter Eight: Where Will You Spend Your Time?

Boyer, Richard, and David Savageau. *Retirement Places Rated.* Chicago, IL: Rand McNally, 1987.

Pierskalla, Carol. *Rehearsal for Retirement.* Valley Forge, PA: National Ministries, American Baptist Churches, USA, 1992.

Chapter Nine: Looking to the Future

"Consumer Guide to Life Care Communities" ($3 pamphlet), the National Consumer League, 1522 K. St. N.W., Suite 406, Washington, DC 20006.

The Gadget Book: Ingenious Devices for Easier Living. Dennis R. LaBuda, ed. Washington, DC: AARP/Scott, Foresman & Co., 1985. This book describes adaptive devices for the home and tells where to find them.

How to Select a Nursing Home, U.S. Dept. of Health and Human Services, Health Care Financing Administration, Consumer Information Center, P.O. Box 100, Pueblo, CO 81002.

Kraus, Anneta S. *Guide to Supportive Living Arrangements for Older Citizens*. Geriatric Planning Services, 116 W. Possum Hollow Rd., Wallingford, PA 19086.

National Continuing Care Directory. Washington, DC: AARP/Scott, Foresman & Co., 1984. Profiles more than 365 life-care communities in thirty-nine states.

Shared Housing Resource Center, 6344 Green St., Philadelphia, PA 19144.

Your Home; Your Choice: A Workbook for Older People and Their Families; Housing Options for Older Americans; The Doable, Renewable Home; and *Home Made Money* (explains home equity conversions), AARP Fulfillment, EE0094, 1909 K St. N.W., Washington, DC 20049.

Chapter Eleven: When You Become the Surviving Spouse

Deane, Barbara. *Caring for Your Aging Parents: When Love Is Not Enough*. Colorado Springs, CO: NavPress, 1989.

Felder, Leonard. *When a Loved One Is Ill: How to Take Better Care of Your Loved One, Your Family and Yourself*. New York: New American Library, 1990.

Loewinsohn, Ruth Jean. *Survival Handbook for Widows (And for Relatives and Friends Who Want to Understand)*. Washington, DC: AARP/ Scott, Foresman & Co., 1987.

Moench, Cynthia L. *Binding Up the Broken-Hearted: A Handbook of Hope for the Chronically Ill & Disabled*. Joplin, MO: College Press, 1991.

The Social Security Book: What Every Woman Absolutely Needs to Know, AARP, 1909 K St. N.W., Washington, DC 20049.

Chapter Twelve: The Enduring Power of Friendships

Crohan, Susan, and Toni C. Antonucci. *Older Adult Friendships*. Rebecca G. Adams and Rosemary Blieszner, eds. Newbury Park, CA: Sage Publications, 1989.

Chapter Thirteen: Once a Parent, Always a Parent

Bloomfield, Harold, and Leonard Felder. *Making Peace with Your Parents*. New York: Random House, 1983.

Graham, Ruth Bell. *Prodigals and Those Who Love Them*. Colorado Springs, CO: Focus on the Family, 1991.

White, Jerry and Mary. *When Your Kids Aren't Kids Anymore*. Colorado Springs, CO: NavPress, 1989.

Chapter Fourteen: Let Your Children Know Who You Are

"Generations" (a game), Generations, Inc., P.O. Box 40169, St. Louis, MO 63141.

Leman, Dr. Kevin, and Randy Carlson. *Unlocking the Secrets of Your Childhood Memories*. Nashville, TN: Thomas Nelson, 1989.

Reminisce (magazine), Reiman Publications, P.O. Box 3088, Milwaukee, WI 53201.

Sheridan, Carmel. *Reminiscence, The Key to Healthy Aging*. San Francisco, CA: Elder Press, 1991.

Chapter Fifteen: Being There for Your Grandchildren

Arizona State University, Robert D. Strom, Professor of Psychology, Tempe, AZ 85287-0112, offers a twelve-week course on how to become a better grandparent.

Foundation for Grandparenting, P.O. Box 31, Lake Placid, NY 12946. For a free copy of their newsletter, send a legal-size SASE (self-addressed, stamped envelope).

Grandparents Against Immorality and Neglect (grandparents' support/advocacy group), c/o Betty Parbs, 720 Kingstown Pl., Shreveport, LA 71108.

Grandparents as Parents, c/o Sylvie de Toledo, Psychiatric Clinic for Youth, 2801 Atlantic Ave., Long Beach, CA 90801.

Grandparents Raising Grandchildren, c/o Barbara Kirkland, P.O. Box 104, Colleyville, TX 76034. (Enclose legal-size SASE.)

Kornhaber, Arthur. *Between Parents and Grandparents*. Berkeley, CA: Berkeley Publications, 1987.

Kornhaber, Arthur, and Kenneth L. Woodward. *Grandparents-Grandchildren: The Vital Connection*. New York: Doubleday, 1981.

Strom, Robert D. and Shirley K. *Becoming a Better Grandparent: A Guidebook for Strengthening the Family* and *Becoming a Better Grandparent: Viewpoints on Strengthening the Family*. Newbury

Park, CA: Sage Publications, 1991.

White, Spike and Darnell. *I Need You: Being Friends with Your Grandkids*. Sisters, OR: Questar Publishers, 1989. Out of print, but copies may still be available from the authors: c/o Kanakuk-Kanakomo Kamps, Rte. 4, Box 2124, Branson, MO 65615.

Chapter Sixteen: The Challenge of Long-Distance Grandparenting

National Association for the Preservation and Perpetuation of Storytelling, P.O. Box 309, Jonesborough, TN 37659, offers a book catalog, newsletter, and list of storytelling festivals.

Chapter Seventeen: What You Can't Afford Not to Know

Albrecht, Donna. *Deals and Discounts If You're 50 or Older*. San Leandro, CA: Bristol Publications, 1990.

Blue, Ron. *Master Your Money*, revised ed. Nashville, TN: Thomas Nelson, 1991.

Complete and Easy Guide to Social Security and Medicare. Burlington, VT: Fraser Publishing Co., 1982. Revised annually. Offers more detailed information than the free Social Security Administration pamphlets.

ERISA (Employment Retirement Security Act), the Pension Benefit Guaranty Corporation, a nonprofit insurance fund, provides protection under some circumstances when pension funds go broke. If you have a question about failure of your pension plan, contact the PBGC at 2020 St. N.W., Washington, DC 20006.

Guide to Health Insurance for People with Medicare (free), *Hospice Benefits Under Medicare* (free), *Medicare and Prepayment Plans* (free), and *The Medicare Handbook* ($2.25), U.S. government publications, Consumer Information Center, P.O. Box 100, Pueblo, CO 81002.

Heilman, Joan Rattner. *Unbelievably Good Deals and Great Adventures That You Absolutely Can't Get Unless You're Over 50*. Chicago, IL: Contemporary Books, 1988.

Matthews, Joseph L. *Social Security, Medicare and Pensions*. Berkeley, CA: Nolo Press, 1990.

Moore, Gary D. *The Thoughtful Christian's Guide to Investing*. Grand Rapids, MI: Zondervan, 1991.

More Health for Your Dollar: An Older Person's Guide to HMOs, and *Choosing an HMO: An Evaluation Checklist,* AARP Fulfillment, 1909 K St. N.W., Washington, DC 20049.

Pension Rights Center, 918 - 16th St. N.W., Washington, DC 20006 (1-202-296-3776), organized to protect and promote pension rights of workers, retirees, and their families. Its Women's Pension Project has published a book entitled *Your Pension Rights at Divorce: What Women Need to Know* ($14.95). The center also answers questions on pension rights.

Quinn, Jane Bryant. *Making the Most of Your Money.* New York: Simon & Schuster, 1991.

Social Security Administration. *A Guide to Social Security Retirement Benefits, A Guide to the Medicare Program, A Guide to Social Security Survivors' Benefits,* and *A Guide to the SSA Program* (1-800-772-1213).

Social Security Explained. Chicago, IL: Commerce Clearing House, revised annually. Offers more detailed information than the free Social Security Administration pamphlets.

Chapter Eighteen: Investing for an Unknown Future

Forbes and *Money* are two magazines to consider. There are many other good finance, business, and investment magazines and newspapers. Many of them you can find in your local library.

Matthews, Joseph L. *Elder Care: Choosing & Financing Long-Term Care.* Berkeley, CA: Nolo Press, 1990.

National Academy of Elder Law Attorneys, 655 N. Alvernon Way, Suite 108, Tucson, AZ 87511. Write for specialists in elder law in your area.

U.S. government booklets, available from Consumer Information Center, P.O. Box 100, Pueblo, CO 81002: *Staying Independent: Planning for Financial Independence in Later Life,* no. 440X ($.50); *Consumer Credit Handbook,* no. 430X ($.50); *Facts About Financial Planners,* no. 434X ($.50); *Investment Swindles: How They Work and How to Avoid Them,* no. 548X (free); and *Money Matters,* no. 442X ($.50). Also see the U.S. Consumer Information Catalog in your public library.

Women's Financial Information Program, the Women's Initiative, AARP, 1909 K St., Washington, DC 20049, has an excellent seven-week course that covers all aspects of money management, not just investments. It's given at various times and places throughout the country—for women only. The course supplies *A Money Management Workbook.*

Chapter Twenty: An Ounce of Prevention

Age Pages, the National Institute on Aging, P.O. Box 8057, Gaithersburg, MD 20898-8057, offers health information on a variety of topics. Request information on the specific health topic you're interested in (free).

Berland, Theodore. *Fitness for Life: Exercises for People Over 50.* Washington, DC: AARP/Scott, Foresman & Co., 1990.

Brody, Jane. *Jane Brody's Good Food Book: Living the High Carbohydrate Way with 350 Recipes.* New York: Bantam Books, 1985.

Chalker, Rebecca, and Kristine E. Whitemore. *Overcoming Bladder Disorders.* New York: Harper & Row, 1990.

Dartmouth Institute for Better Health. *Medical and Health Guide for People Over Fifty.* Washington, DC: AARP/Scott, Foresman & Co., 1989.

Feltin, Marie. *A Woman's Guide to Good Health After 50.* Washington, DC: AARP/Scott, Foresman & Co., 1991.

Graedon, Joe and Teresa. *50+: The Graedons' People's Pharmacy for Older Adults.* New York: Bantam, 1988.

Hartmann, Ernest. *The Sleep Book: Understanding and Preventing Sleep Problems in People Over 50.* Washington, DC: AARP/Scott, Foresman & Co., 1990.

Katcher, Brian S. *Prescription Drugs: An Indispensable Guide for People Over 50.* New York: Avon, 1988.

Managing Incontinence. Simon Foundation, P.O. Box 815, Wilmette, IL 60091. (Public information hot line, 1-800-23-SIMON.)

Ornish, Dean. *Stress, Diet and Your Heart.* New York: Henry Holt & Co., 1982. Also contains recipes.

Ralston, Jeannie. *Walking for the Health of It: The Easy and Effective Exercise for People Over 50.* Washington, DC: AARP/Scott, Foresman & Co., 1991.

Robertson, Laurel; Flinders, Carol; and Godfrey, Bronwen. *Laurel's Kitchen: A Handbook for Vegetarian Cooker and Nutrition.* Petaluma, CA: Nilgiri Press, 1976.

USDA dietary guideline bulletins #HG 232-8 and #HG 232-1-11, Consumer Information Center, P.O. Box 100, Pueblo, CO 81002.

Chapter Twenty-One: Strengthening Your Spiritual Muscles

Boomershine, Thomas E. *Story Journey: An Invitation to the Gospel as Storytelling*. Nashville, TN: Abingdon Press, 1988.

Davis, Ron Lee. *Mentoring: The Strategy of the Master*. Nashville, TN: Thomas Nelson, 1991.

Dewey, Kirk. *Stories: God's Hand in My Life*. Swarthmore, PA: Support Source, 1990.

Fischer, Kathleen. *Winter Grace: Spirituality for the Later Years*. Mahwah, NJ: Paulist Press, 1985.

Foster, Richard J. *Celebration of Discipline*, rev. ed. San Francisco, CA: Harper & Row, 1988.

Geissler, Eugene S. *The Best Is Yet to Be: Life's Meaning in the Aging Years*. Notre Dame, IN: Ave Maria Press, 1988.

Moench, Cynthia L. *Binding Up the Broken Hearted: A Handbook of Hope for the Chronically Ill and Disabled*. Joplin, MO: College Press, 1991.

Morgan, Richard L. *No Wrinkles on the Soul: A Book of Readings for Older Adults*. Nashville, TN: The Upper Room, 1990.

Rupp, Joyce. *Praying Our Goodbyes*. Notre Dame, IN: Ave Maria Press, 1988.

Soth, Connie. *Insomnia, God's Night School*. Old Tappan, NJ: Fleming H. Revell, 1989.

Wakefield, Daniel. *The Story of Your Life: Writing a Spiritual Autobiography*. Boston, MA: Beacon Press, 1990.

Whitney, Donald S. *Spiritual Disciplines for the Christian Life*. Colorado Springs, CO: NavPress, 1991.

NOTES

Introduction

1. Ken Dytchtwald, Ph.D., and Joe Flower, *Age Wave: The Challenges and Opportunities of an Aging America* (Los Angeles, CA: Jeremy P. Tarcher, 1989), page 4.

Chapter One: Getting to Know Me

1. Eugene C. Bianchi, *Aging as a Spiritual Journey* (New York: Crossroad Publishing Co., 1982), page 193.
2. Eda LeShan, *Oh, To Be 50 Again!* (New York: New York Times Books, 1986), page 60.
3. Viktor Frankl, "Facing the Transitoriness of Human Existence," *Generations, Quarterly Journal of the American Society on Aging,* vol. XIV, no. 4, Fall 1990, page 9.

Chapter Two: Letting Go

1. Ken Dytchtwald, Ph.D., and Joe Flower, *Age Wave: The Challenges and Opportunities of an Aging America* (Los Angeles, CA: Jeremy P. Tarcher, 1989), page 27.

Chapter Three: Planning to Grow

1. The phrase "Elders of the Tribe" as a role for the aging in our society was first suggested by Maggie Kuhn, founder of

the Gray Panthers.

2. George E. Vaillant, M.D., and Carolyn O. Vaillant, MSSW, "Natural History of Male Psychological Health, XII, a 45-Year Study of Predictors of Successful Aging at Age 65," *American Journal of Psychiatry,* vol. 147, no. 1, January 1990, pages 31-37.
3. Viktor Frankl, "Facing the Transitoriness of Human Existence," *Generations, Quarterly Journal of the American Society on Aging,* vol. XIV, no. 4, Fall 1990, page 9.

Chapter Four: Time for Exploration and Discovery

1. Thomas Merton, *No Man Is an Island* (New York: Harcourt, Brace, Jovanovich, 1955), pages 28-29.

Chapter Five: Volunteering: Finding Yourself by Giving Yourself Away

1. Susan Maizel Chambre, *Good Deeds in Old Age: Volunteering by the New Leisure Class* (Lexington, MA: Lexington Books, 1987), page 5.

Chapter Seven: If You Need Paid Employment

1. Caroline Bird, "The Jobs You Dream About: What Seniors Want in a Second Career," *Modern Maturity,* February-March 1988, pages 31-37.

Chapter Eight: Where Will You Spend Your Time?

1. Richard Boyer and David Savageau, *Retirement Places Rated* (Chicago: Rand McNally, 1987).
2. *Senior Spectrum,* May 10, 1990, page 9.
3. Arthur Kornhaber, M.D., and Kenneth L. Woodward, *Grandparents, Grandchildren, the Vital Connection* (New York: Doubleday, 1981), page 243.
4. Kornhaber and Woodward, page 97.
5. Carol Spargo Pierskalla, *Rehearsal for Retirement* (Valley Forge, PA: American Baptist Church, 1991), page 18.

Chapter Ten: The Post-Retirement Marriage

1. Margaret Clark, "The Anthropology of Aging: A New Area for Studies of Culture and Personality," *The Gerontologist,* vol. 8, no. 1, March 1967.

2. Paul Fremont Brown, *From Here to Retirement* (Waco, TX: Word Books, 1988), page 187.

Chapter Eleven: When You Become the Surviving Spouse

1. AARP, *How to Plan Your Successful Retirement,* page 50; and Beth B. Hess, "Gender and Aging: The Demographic Parameters," *Generations,* Summer 1990, pages 12-15. Statistics used are 1989 U.S. Bureau of Census figures.
2. Marjorie Fiske Lowenthal and Clayton Haven, "Interaction and Adaptation: Intimacy as a Critical Variable," in *Middle Age and Aging: A Reader in Social Psychology,* ed. Bernice L. Neugarten (Chicago: University of Chicago Press, 1968).
3. 1983 U.S. Census.

Chapter Twelve: The Enduring Power of Friendships

1. Ethel Shanas, et al., "The Psychology of Health," in *Middle Age and Aging: A Reader in Social Psychology,* ed. Bernice L. Neugarten (Chicago: University of Chicago Press, 1968), page 217.
2. Sarah H. Matthews, *Friendship Throughout the Life Course* (Newbury Park, CA: Sage Library of Social Research, 1986), pages 33-58.
3. Jamie Quackenbush, MSW, and Denise Graveline, *When Your Pet Dies: How to Cope with Your Feelings* (New York: Simon & Schuster, 1985), page 121.

Chapter Thirteen: Once a Parent, Always a Parent

1. Quoted in *Senior Spectrum,* July 5, 1990, page 4.
2. Alice Duer Miller, in *Quotable Women, A Collection of Shared Thoughts* (Philadelphia, PA: Running Press, 1989), page 80.
3. For more information on Erikson and his theories, see Robert Coles, *Erik H. Erikson: The Growth of His Work* (Boston: Little, Brown, 1970). For a discussion of his theories as they apply in later life, see Erik H. Erikson, *Vital Involvement in Old Age* (New York: Norton, 1986).

Chapter Fourteen: Let Your Children Know Who You Are

1. I'm indebted to my friend Helen Hight for passing on this questionnaire, which was given to her by a family member. I have shortened and adapted it. Its original author is unknown to us.

Chapter Fifteen: Being There for Your Grandchildren

1. Arthur Kornhaber, M.D., and Kenneth L. Woodward, *Grandparents, Grandchildren, the Vital Connection* (Doubleday, 1981), page 55.
2. Eda LeShan, "Grandparents Get a Second Chance," *Senior Spectrum*, June 7, 1990, page 2.
3. Arthur Kornhaber, M.D., *Between Parents and Grandparents* (New York: St. Martin's Press, 1986), page 12.
4. Kornhaber and Woodward, page xxii.
5. Vern L. Bengtson and Joan F. Robertson, eds., *Grandparenthood* (Newbury Park, CA: Sage Publications, 1985), pages 37-38.
6. Spike and Darnell White, *I Need You: Being Friends with Your Grandkids* (Sisters, OR: Questar, 1989), page 40.

Chapter Eighteen: Investing for an Unknown Future

1. The risk is not losing the principal, but losing income due to falling interest rates.
2. See Proverbs 27:23-24.
3. Ron Blue, *Master Your Money: A Step-by-Step Plan for Financial Freedom* (Nashville, TN: Thomas Nelson, 1986), page 198.
4. See 2 Peter 2:3.
5. See Ecclesiastes 11:1.
6. See Ecclesiastes 11:2.
7. See Proverbs 20:23.
8. For a more detailed account of how swindlers prey on the older person, see the April-May 1991 issue of *Modern Maturity*, pages 31-44.
9. Reported in *Woman's Day*, January 15, 1991, page 64.

Chapter Nineteen: Attitude Is Everything

1. Kathleen Fischer, *Winter Grace, Spirituality for the Later Years* (Mahwah, NJ: Paulist Press, 1985), pages 101-102.
2. This research is reported by Ethel Shanas, et al., "The Psychology of Health," in *Middle Age and Aging: A Reader in Social Psychology*, ed. Bernice L. Neugarten (Chicago, IL: University of Chicago Press, 1968), page 212.
3. Robert N. Butler, M.D., "The Face of Chronological Age," in *Middle Age and Aging: A Reader in Social Psychology*, ed.

Bernice L. Neugarten (Chicago: University of Chicago Press, 1968), page 217.

4. Timothy A. Salthouse, "Cognitive Facets of Aging Well," *Generations,* Winter 1991, page 36.

Chapter Twenty: An Ounce of Prevention

1. Ken Dytchtwald, Ph.D., and Joe Flower, *Age Wave: The Challenges and Opportunities of an Aging America* (Los Angeles, CA: Jeremy P. Tarcher, 1989), page xvi, emphasis added.
2. Jay Sokolovsky and Marie D. Vesperi, "The Cultural Context of Well-Being in Old Age," *Generations,* Winter 1991, page 21.
3. Dean Ornish, M.D., *Stress, Diet and Your Heart* (New York: Henry Holt & Co., 1984), page 6.
4. John W. Rowe, M.D., "Reducing the Risk of Usual Aging," *Generations,* Winter 1991, page 26.
5. Results of a study of family practice physicians' attitudes toward middle age, commissioned by the American Board of Family Practice. Announced in a press release from the American Board of Family Practice in 1990.
6. Office of Disease Prevention and Health Promotion, Public Health Service, U.S. Department of Health and Human Services Program Memo, "Healthy Older People," 1990.
7. Maria A. Fiatarone, M.D., et al., "High-Intensity Strength Training in Nonagenarians," *JAMA,* June 13, 1990, vol. 263, no. 22, pages 3029-3034.
8. For additional information, see an article entitled "A Pyramid Topples at the USDA," published in *Consumer Reports,* October 1991, pages 663-666.

Chapter Twenty-One: Strengthening Your Spiritual Muscles

1. Jane J. Thibault, "The Spiritual Call of Later Life: Finding God Within," *Weavings,* January-February 1991, page 12.
2. Ron Lee Davis, *Mentoring, the Strategy of the Master* (Nashville: Thomas Nelson, 1991).
3. Davis, page 214.
4. Kirk Dewey, *Stories: God's Hand in My Life* (Swarthmore, PA: Support Source, 1991), page 22.
5. Daniel Wakefield, *The Story of Your Life: Writing a Spiritual Autobiography* (Boston: Beacon Press, 1990), page 25.

6. Thomas E. Boomershine, *Story Journey: An Invitation to the Gospel as Storytelling* (Nashville, TN: Abbington Press, 1988), pages 67-68.
7. Richard J. Foster, *Celebration of Discipline: The Path to Spiritual Growth* (New York: Harper & Row, revised ed. 1988).
8. Foster, pages 22-23.
9. *The Golden Years* (Littleton, CO: Serendipity, 1991), page 97.
10. Foster, page 96.
11. Connie Soth, *Insomnia, God's Night School* (Old Tappan, NJ: Fleming H. Revell, 1989), pages 23-26.
12. Joyce Rupp, *Praying Our Goodbyes* (Notre Dame, IN: Ave Maria Press, 1988), page 57.

INDEX

AUTHOR

Barbara Deane, author of *Caring for Your Aging Parents: When Love Is Not Enough,* is a writer, lecturer, and workshop leader on issues of caregiving and aging. A member of the American Society of Journalists and Authors and the American Society on Aging, she has been a freelance writer for almost twenty years. Her work has appeared in *Ladies Home Journal, Woman's Day, Family Circle, Reader's Digest, Virtue,* and many other publications.

In 1984, as a result of caring for her aging mother, Barbara co-founded Christian Caregivers Support Group, which continues to meet the needs of the families of the elderly in her community. The book she wrote out of this experience, *Caring for Your Aging Parents: When Love Is Not Enough,* published by NavPress in 1989, has been hailed as an "essential handbook" by caregivers, pastors, social workers, and medical professionals who work with the elderly and their families.